TOP CHEFS TOP RECIPES

Anil Bhandari

Popular Prakashan
www.popularprakashan.com

Published by
POPULAR PRAKASHAN PVT. LTD.
301, Mahalaxmi Chambers
22, Bhulabhai Desai Road
Mumbai – 400 026
for KHANA KHAZANA PUBLICATIONS PVT. LTD.

First Published 2014

(4369)
ISBN: 978-81-7991-810-4

Spice sketches: Mulchand Panchal
Cartoon sketches: Sudhir Dar
Design: Mahendra Ghanekar, Anjali Sawant
Photography: Bharat Bhirangi, Sanjeev Nadkarni, Satish Parab,
Swapnil Naik, Vikas Shinde

Printed in India
by Infinity Advertising Services Pvt. Ltd.
D – 4/2, Okhla Industrial Area Phase-1
New Delhi 110020

To
all the
chefs of
Hotels
&
Restaurants
of India

Contents

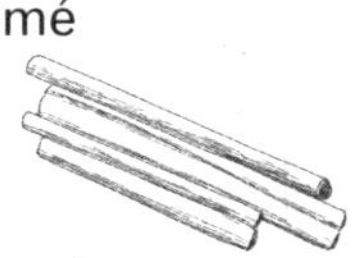

RICE & BREAD

ACCOMPANIMENTS

SWEETS & DESSERTS

Preface

French, Italian and Chinese cuisines are known all over the world. Even American junk food is easily available, from Spanish beachfronts to Beijing's upmarket areas. Most restaurants which serve Indian cuisine, however, are confined to Indian-dominated areas overseas. Cuisines from several other countries such as Japan and Korea have also not achieved widespread acceptance.

India is light years ahead of other countries in terms of the wealth and range of its cuisines, availability and fusion of exotic spices, cooking legends as well as techniques. The Western world has historically been aware of India's exotic spices. Visitors to India have been known to blend their bland gastronomical fare with Indian spices, and in the process adding to the rich repertoire of Indian cuisine.

India's 5,000 year old history and rich heritage continues to be a subject of widespread research. With a population exceeding 1.2 billion that resides in 640 districts across 29 states and 7 Union Territories over a total land mass of 3,287,263 square kilometres and a coastline of over 7,517 kilometres, it is natural that the flavours of India's culinary diversities, traditions and preferences are immense.

People adhering to different religious beliefs such as Hindus, Muslims, Sikhs, Christians, Jains, Parsis and Buddhists follow their particular culinary-cum-religious values in terms of food, recipes and cooking techniques. The four seasons add to the variety and choice of seasonal fruit and vegetables. Recipes meant for the summer are lighter than those for the winters. Different geographical locations also govern the cooking patterns of the populace. Inhabitants of coastal regions have cuisines using fish and coconut or mustard, while lamb and chicken dominate the cuisines of colder climes.

Food has always been accorded a special status in India's social fabric. Religious festivals, social functions or family get-togethers are all occasions for serving traditional food items linked to such events. A birth in the family is announced by distributing *laddu*. *Gujiya* and *seviyan ki kheer* are an inherent part of Holi and Id-ul-Fitr respectively.

What does one say about Indian food? It ignites all the five senses, it is a treat for the eyes, a captivating fragrance, a memorable taste, a titillation of the palate and nourishment for the body. Customarily eaten with the fingers, it acquires spiritual connotations. India has such an incredibly large variety of cuisines that we have not been able to research, standardise and publish a definitive compendium of our country's recipes. What is available at present are stand-alone recipe books based on state and regional cuisines; vegetarian and non-vegetarian delicacies; desserts and health foods.

India does not have a definitive compendium of recipes like the legendary Frenchman Georges Auguste Escoffier's *Le Guide Culinaire* published in 1903 which continues to be used as a major reference, both as a cookbook and as a textbook on cooking not only in France, but all across the world.

A large number of Indian cuisines have still not been documented and remain confined to remote pockets across the country. India needs to produce a compendium of recipes or a cookbook that will help promote Indian cuisine and its distinctive cooking techniques all over the world, thereby leading to the ascendance of extraordinary chefs.

Promotion of India's myriad cuisines and propagating our culinary arts will enable tourists to sample and familiarise themselves with exotic Indian cuisines. I recognise the charisma of Indian cuisine. The variety, variations, skills, colours, flavours, aromas that can be conjured up by a chef, depending on the regional style he utilises, are infinite. The richness of Indian cuisine is unsurpassable. Our cuisine is one of the manifold reasons that make India truly incredible.

I am a connoisseur of good food. I have travelled extensively and have developed an appreciation for food from all corners of the globe. I have compiled this book of recipes with a view to share the knowledge of the process of converting ingredients into appetising and delicious dishes. I want to popularise Indian food internationally, and therefore this book showcases Indian recipes.

The recipes in this book were prepared by renowned chefs of the Ashok Group of Hotels, Centaur Hotels as well as many other kitchens and my fellow colleagues who worked with me. A question arises: "What are the key characteristics of a good chef?" A chef, in my considered view has to be an artist, a scientist, a finance and human resources manager, all rolled into one. Like an artist the chef has to create a variety of dishes which not only taste good but are also attractively presented and give out irresistible aromas.

A chef needs to have a multidimensional personality and skills. He should be able to stand for long hours in the kitchen and get acclimatised to the heat emanating from the burners and ovens. A chef needs to master the art of working in teams and meeting compressed deadlines, round-the-clock. A chef has to have considerable patience and work like an artist.

A chef needs to proceed scientifically while preparing a nutritious meal, calculate the exact portion and combination of various ingredients to obtain the right flavour and know how to preserve food and raw stock. A chef also needs to control costs, inventory and finances to ensure profitability of the enterprise.

The recipes included in this book can be prepared using simple cooking techniques at home. This book is a way to figuratively share my knowledge, experiences and tastes with the readers, as well as a means to compliment my fellow colleagues for their cooperation and to express my heartfelt thanks to all my teachers.

I learnt the basics of the business of cooking at my alma mater, the Institute of Hotel Management, Pusa, New Delhi. During my three-year stint at the Institute of Hotel Management, I imbibed the knowledge of commodity, nutrition, hygiene, Continental and Indian cuisine, bakery, confectionary as well as bulk cooking and I must have cooked over 1,000 recipes.

The recipes in this book are an integral part of my experiences in a career spanning a period of over 44 years or 12,900 man days or 103,200 hours. I would like to recount some incidents which occurred during those years, days and hours.

After finishing my studies at the Institute of Hotel Management, Pusa I joined India Tourism Development Corporation and was posted at the hotels in Bodh-Gaya, Bhubaneshwar, Konark, New Delhi's Ashok Hotel and finally at the Bangalore Ashok where I got the opportunity to look after the rooftop restaurant Kohinoor, then the best restaurant in the Garden City. Bangalore then had not become the hi-tech city it is today.

The view from the rooftop restaurant, specialising in Continental food, was peaceful. My specialisation, of flambé preparations, did not permit me to enjoy the view for long as many guests would request me to prepare dishes such as Steak Diane, Pepper Steak, Peach Flambé and Crêpe Suzette.

The guests ranged from the State Governor, the Chief Minister, the famous pioneer J.R.D. Tata, industrialists such as the Khodays and Mallyas, to film actors like Sanjay Khan, Rajesh Khanna, Dimple Kapadia and many more leading personalities.

After Bangalore I went for specialised training to West Germany. I opted to work in the kitchen at the Mainz Hilton. On the first day I was posted to the butchery department where carcasses of buffaloes, pigs, fish, chicken and other animals had to be cleaned and cut into portions as per the requirements of various departments. Hilton had a large banqueting facility and during the weeklong Mainz Carnival over 1,500 people would come for their evening meals in two shifts. That meant a total of 3,000 meals.

For the preparation of cold cuts, I was assigned to prepare sausages. That task took the entire day and for three days I made only sausages. Thereafter, for the next three days I was transferred to the Hot Kitchen where I was assigned to sauté sausages. At the end of a long day of hard work, my dreams, often, were about sausages galore!

In the Patisserie department I learnt a lot about confectionary and the art of how to prepare various kinds of breads, croissants and desserts, pastries and cakes such as the Black Forest cake. My instructor-chef would send me to the store daily to get a bottle of cherry liqueur. Half the contents of the bottle were mixed in the batter and the remaining half would go down my instructor's throat!

A major learning experience was when I was General Manager/Vice-president of catering of the Prime Minister's Guest House, Hyderabad House, for over three years, I had the privilege of looking after State banquets which were hosted for visiting Presidents, Prime Ministers and other dignitaries by various Prime Ministers such as Smt. Indira Gandhi, Shri Morarji Desai, Shri A.B. Vajpayee, Shri Deve Gowda, Shri I.K. Gujral and Shri Rajiv Gandhi. According to the demands of the occasion, we would serve the choicest dishes prepared for royalty. Some of these recipes have been included in this book.

I was also responsible for the catering of 91 Heads of State who attended the Non-Aligned Meeting in 1983 at Vigyan Bhavan. It was a test of my skill as we had to cater to each Head of State as per his dietary requirements, as prescribed by his country's representative. Smt. Indira Gandhi, and later Shri Rajiv Gandhi, were very particular about the food served at important functions.

Another assignment I am proud of was the kitchen planning for the hotels of the Ashok Group. It involved creation of a Food and Beverage concept followed by area-planning which involved a time-and-motion study before drawing up the kitchen plans. It was a daunting task as a lot of kitchen equipment was not available in India.

So I picked up ideas from kitchen company catalogues, made drawings of the items with the help of Indian equipment manufacturers like 'Continental Equipment' and 'Thakkar Equipment' and got the items made in India. This tendency to innovate and improvise became a routine with me later.

I did the kitchen planning for the Ashok Hotels at Agra, Bhubaneswar, Varanasi, Patliputra Ashok in Patna, Jammu Ashok, Khajuraho Ashok, Bangalore Ashok, Lalitha Mahal Palace in Mysore, Hasan Ashok, Karnavati Ashok in Ahmedabad, New Delhi's Ashok Yatri Nivas, Kanishka and Vigyan Bhavan as well as the planning for hotels in Dokan and Mosul in Iraq and Limasol in Cyprus.

I was in-charge of kitchen planning and design for the Asian Games held in 1982. A prestigious event, the planning of 8,000 meals daily for athletes, needed to be done on a colossal scale. The meals, comprising Indian, Chinese and Continental cuisines, were to be planned as per specifications laid down by the Asian Games authorities and nutritionists of participating countries. Accordingly, we had to plan and order the required raw material and the kitchen equipment such as boilers, grillers, fryers, etc.

For the Games' kitchen it was decided to buy equipment which could be utilised subsequently by India Tourism Development Corporation in its various hotels. Keeping this in mind, the equipment bought was of lower capacity. For instance, 16 potato peelers, each of which could peel 20 kg of potatoes per hour were bought instead of the 50 kg per hour peelers.

The Games kitchen was the biggest ever planned till then in the country. My planning was studied and approved by foreign chefs and the kitchen planner Mr. Lief Torne. Considering the size of the equipment, the suppliers, Electrolux, dispatched the entire consignment from Sweden to India in a Jumbo plane. Today Doordarshan studios occupy the space where the Games kitchen once stood.

At ITDC's Kanishka Hotel during the Asian Games, we created special sports-theme dishes which were served at the Palm Court restaurant for the duration of the Games. On this special occasion even the table mats had cartoons with images of sports events and related captions. The 'Bread Basket' cartoon represented basketball, 'Pizza from South' lampooned the *uthapam* being used as a discus, while 'Nawab Kabab' showed a relay race baton change in progress with Seekh Kababs being used as the batons. These cartoons are highlighted in the book were commissioned by me. We would like our readers to share the pleasure given to all of us by the eminent cartoonist Sudhir Dar.

During the Asian Games a unique menu was created to give competition to Machan, the Taj Mansingh Hotel's coffee shop. The menu included Honey Bunch which was strawberry milk shake sweetened with honey, and Fruit Delight, a concoction of juices and a fruit served chilled. As was Pussycat, a colourful layered drink made by carefully pouring Rooh Afza, followed by mango juice, and pineapple juice, and finally Fanta on top in a tall glass.

Today considered common, many of the dishes we created, including the Nawab Kabab, a special Seekh Kabab served on a bed of rice with mutton curry gravy and *kachumber*, were a novelty in that era.

We also took the initiative and introduced combo meals such as the above-mentioned Nawab Kabab, Rajmah-Rice, and Vegetable au-gratin with rice cooked in curry sauce. A unique dessert item and in great demand was the Ice Cream Sandwich, made by encasing a slice of vanilla ice cream between two slices of chocolate cake.

Another innovation was the soup we offered with bread rolls and bread sticks in a basket made out of the same dough as the rolls and bread sticks. Some of our soups were innovative, with a fusion of distinctive and unusual combinations. Some of these were Tomato Broth and cold soups such as Aam Panna and Cold Cucumber Soup.

I was also involved with the promotion of Indian cuisine at the Festivals of India held in the United States of America, both at Washington and New York; as also in the Malaysian capital, Kuala Lumpur.

In Washington we had created the concept of a *dhaba* (roadside eatery), to be set up on the lawns in front of the Smithsonian Museum. Serving over

1,500 meals from 11 a.m. to 4 p.m. every day, we used up 1,000 chickens and 200 litres of yogurt, daily. As we had no idea of American food hygiene standards, another surprise for us was the stationing of doctors at our kitchen to check the food temperatures.

Soon after this event, Sant Chatwal opened his restaurant, the Bombay Palace in Washington and the Indian food served at the restaurant became popular overnight with dignitaries such as the then US President Bill Clinton and his family dining there.

Prior to the Festival of India we sent a team of chefs during a state visit by the then Prime Minister, Shri Rajiv Gandhi, to the US Vice-President. Serving Indian preparations at the Kennedy Center was a difficult task. Security men stood around the tables during the service and every dish taken from the kitchen to the dining room was manually checked with metal detectors.

The Food and Beverage Department is the backbone of a hotel. At the Ashok Group and Centaur Group we would organise in-house international or regional cuisine festivals every month. The planning for this was done in the beginning of the year with the cooperation of the chefs and marketing executives. Taken into consideration were national, regional, seasonal events as well as religious festivals.

Recipes for the regional cuisine would be obtained through research and in consultation with housewives belonging to the State. For the international variety, authentic recipes would be obtained from the concerned embassies or high commissions. Japanese, Chinese, Spanish, Italian, Greek, Burmese were some of the festivals which were highly appreciated.

I had worked as a startup General Manager for a number of new Ashok Group of Hotels and had developed interest in cookery while working at the ITDC. Even when I was Chairman and Managing Director of India Tourism Development Corporation as well as Managing Director of Hotel Corporation of India, I would meet with chefs of the hotels.

I would encourage the chefs and F&B managers by conducting cookery competitions. This invariably led to the creation of new dishes, innovative ways to improve the presentation, flavours etc. of their preparations and of course the means to finally standardise recipes. Many of the chefs were keen participants and would cook a new dish on a daily or weekly basis. Celebrity chef Sanjeev Kapoor was one among them.

To motivate chefs all over the country I mooted the idea of organising the chef Awards in the year 2004 with the collaboration of the PHD Chamber of Commerce and Industry. Since then we have been organising chefs' Day annually to honour talented chefs in various disciplines. I persuaded the Ministry of Tourism to recognise the role of chefs in the hospitality industry. As a result, the Ministry of Tourism established two National awards for outstanding chefs of the country since 2008. I continue my efforts to persuade the Government of India to award the Padma Shri and Padma Bhushan to deserving chefs.

Today chefs are visible, with live open kitchens in restaurants where they interact and explain the intricacies of various dishes and field questions from curious diners. Newspapers and magazines have dedicated pages for various cuisines and chefs. Many international and domestic TV channels have cookery shows with chefs displaying their skills.

Being a member of the National Tourism Advisory Council I have convinced the Government of India to set up an Indian Culinary Institute of Arts and Research. The Ministry of Tourism has agreed in principle and is agreeable to develop one such Institute. With four regional chapters, this institute would also conduct research on Indian cuisine and document a large variety of recipes. This would help in the teaching of Indian cuisine in foreign Culinary Institutes and ultimately result in popularising Indian food internationally.

I acknowledge all the chefs and the other staff who helped make my journey into the culinary arts possible - chef Rouger Moncourt, chef Fernandes, chef Sanjeev Kapoor, chef Sudhir Sibal, chef Rosario, chef J.M. Chaudhary, chef K.N. Vinod, chef M.S. Gupta, chef Ramachander, chef Raja Ratnam, chef C.S. Jain, chef Sishir Saxena, chef Bhattacharya, chef Suvan Somani, chef Loomba, chef Vinod Dua, chef Verma, chef Peter Hessen, chef Zurberger, chef Zimmerman, and many more.

Anil Bhandari

Spices (Masala) of India

Indian spices are known the world over for their exotic flavours to culinary preparations. The range of regional cuisines is vast as a result of the variations in the use of spices. Their healing and preventive powers are well documented by proponents of Ayurvedic medicine.

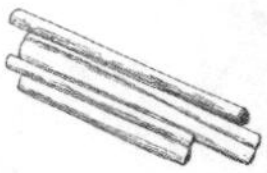

Bishop's weed (*ajwain*): Housewives use bishop's weed seeds as a spice in cooking due to its specific property of improving the digestion of food. The seeds are useful in curing stomach disorders, relieve spasms and have an antiseptic effect in the digestive tract.

Black peppercorns (*kali mirch*): Black pepper, used in the form of berries or powder, adds spice to the food and aids digestion. Among home remedies a decoction of black pepper, dried ginger, clove, cardamom, cinnamon and tea is a deterrent against coughs and colds.

Cinnamon (*dalchini*): The dried inner bark of the cinnamon has an important place in Indian cooking. From ancient times the bark has been used as a home remedy.

Cloves (*laung*): A spice used to add exotic flavour to food, the clove pods are aromatic, appetisers, digestive aids and help in the purification of blood. The pods and the oil extract have medicinal properties both for internal and external use.

Coriander seeds (*sukha dhaniya*): Coriander seeds are a rich source of minerals. Fresh leaves are used for garnishing due to their aroma.

Cumin seed (*jeera*): Giving a distinctive flavour to food, cumin seeds are used in curries and pickles. Its regular usage in food keeps the digestive tract healthy. The seed contains an aromatic volatile oil and is used in medicine.

Fennel (*saunf*): In India, eating a pinch of fennel seeds after a meal is common as it aids digestion. Fennel is used to treat low blood pressure, respiratory congestion and cough.

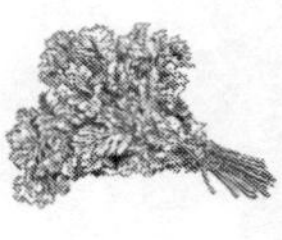

Green cardamom (*chhoti ilaichi*): Cardamom is a very aromatic spice and in combination with other spices is used in adding aroma and taste to Indian cuisine. Cardamom seeds are also used as a flavouring agent.

Mace (*javitri*): Mace is strongly aromatic, resinous and warm in taste. Mace is actually a part of the nutmeg. The bright red, lacy outer covering or shell of nutmeg is called mace. When removed and dried the resulting "blades" of mace have a slightly more delicate but pungent flavour.

Nutmeg (*jaiphal*): A tasty spice, it is used in desserts and in baking. It can help lower blood pressure, calm a stomach ache and help detoxify the body. Nutmeg oil is effective for relieving stress and stimulating mental activity.

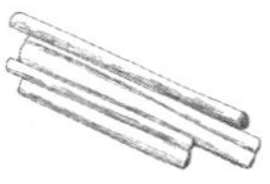

Red chilli powder (*lal mirch* powder): The chilli peppers, source of red chilli powder, are members of the capsicum family, coming in all shapes, sizes, and colours. They have little aroma but vary in taste from mild to fiery hot and enhance the bland flavour of staple foods.

Saffron (*zaffran*): A herb which imparts a special taste, fragrance and colour to food and to sweetmeats, it is also a tonic, stimulant, rejuvenator, appetizer, digestive and anti-spasmodic in nature.

Turmeric (*haldi*): The powder of the turmeric plant's tubers and rhizomes are used to give a mild aroma and a deep yellow-orange colour to foods. A versatile spice, it acts as a tonic, appetiser and astringent.

SOUPS & STARTERS

Palm Court

होटल कनिष्क
Hotel Kanishka

Almond Soup

Ingredients

15-20 almonds
5 cups Vegetable Stock (see below)
1 tablespoon butter
1 tablespoon refined flour (*maida*)
¾ cup hot milk
3-4 drops almond essence
Salt to taste
White pepper powder to taste
2 teaspoons fresh cream

Method

1. Soak the almonds in hot water for ten minutes. Drain and peel them. Keep three almonds aside and blend the remaining in a blender jar with a little vegetable stock.
2. Transfer the almond paste into a bowl, add the remaining vegetable stock and set aside. Chop the reserved almonds into slivers and roast them in an oven till crisp. Set them aside for garnishing.
3. Melt the butter in a deep non-stick pan, add the flour and cook on medium heat for ten to fifteen seconds, taking care that the flour does not change colour.
4. Add the almond paste-stock mixture and mix well so that no lumps remain. Simmer for ten minutes, stirring continuously. Add the hot milk, almond essence, salt and white pepper powder. Mix well and let it simmer for a few seconds.
5. Remove from heat, strain into another pan and add the cream. Mix well.
6. Serve hot, garnished with almond slivers.

• **Preparation time:** 30-35 minutes • **Cooking time:** 30-35 minutes • **Serves:** 4

Vegetable Stock

Vegetable stock also known as white stock can be prepared by boiling five cups of water with 1 chopped onion, ½ cup shredded cabbage, few cauliflower florets, 2 crushed garlic cloves, 5-6 black peppercorns and 1 bay leaf.

Minestrone Soup

Ingredients

1 medium carrot, diced
1 medium turnip (*shalgam*), diced
8-10 French beans, diced
1 leek stalk, diced
2 medium tomatoes, blanched, peeled and chopped
150 grams cabbage, diced
60 grams macaroni, halved
1 tablespoon oil
1 medium onion, chopped
1 garlic clove, chopped
Salt to taste
Black pepper powder to taste
5 cups Vegetable Stock (refer page 16)
2 tablespoons grated cheese

Method

1. Heat the oil in a deep non-stick pan; add the onion, garlic, carrot, turnip and beans and sauté till the onion is translucent.
2. Add the leek, salt, pepper powder, tomatoes and cabbage and mix. Add the vegetable stock.
3. When the soup starts boiling, add the macaroni. Lower the heat; let the soup simmer till the vegetables and macaroni are cooked.
4. Serve, garnished with grated cheese.

• **Preparation time:** 15-20 minutes • **Cooking time:** 20-25 minutes • **Serves:** 4

Green Peas Soup

Ingredients

2 cups shelled green peas
1 cup white sauce
Salt to taste
Black pepper powder to taste

For garnishing
4 teaspoons fresh cream
½ cup bread croutons

Method

1. Boil the peas in a deep non-stick pan with four cups of water.
2. When the peas turn soft, blend them along with the cooking liquid. Strain the blended liquid, add the white sauce, salt and pepper powder and mix well.
3. Before serving, heat the soup and pour into individual soup bowls. Garnish with the fresh cream and bread croutons and serve hot.

• **Preparation time:** 10-15 minutes • **Cooking time:** 15-20 minutes • **Serves:** 4

Carrot And Orange Soup

Ingredients

500 grams carrots, cubed
2 cups orange juice
5 teaspoons butter
1 medium onion, chopped
Salt to taste
⅓ teaspoon white pepper powder
4 teaspoons sugar
2 cups Vegetable Stock (refer page 16)
½ cup fresh cream

Method

1. Heat the butter in a deep non-stick pan; add the onion and sauté till translucent.
2. Add the carrots and sauté for a minute. Add the salt, white pepper powder and sugar and mix. Add the vegetable stock and stir.

3. Cook on low heat till carrots are tender. Remove pan from heat and allow the soup to cool.
4. Line a soup strainer with a piece of muslin and pass the soup through it directly into a deep non-stick pan. Add the orange juice and stir.
5. Stir in the cream and reheat the strained soup for a minute.
6. Remove pan from heat and pour into individual soup bowls. Serve hot.

• **Preparation time:** 30-35 minutes • **Cooking time:** 40-45 minutes • **Serves:** 4

Broccoli And Walnut Soup

Ingredients

400 grams broccoli, separated into florets

6-8 walnut kernels, chopped

2 tablespoons butter

1 medium onion, chopped

2-3 garlic cloves, chopped

1 small leek, chopped

2 inches celery, chopped

Salt to taste

⅓ teaspoon white pepper powder

4 cups Vegetable Stock (refer page 16)

¼ cup cream

Method

1. Heat the butter in a deep non-stick pan. Add the onion and garlic, sauté for a minute.
2. Add the leek, celery, broccoli and mix well. Add salt, white pepper and vegetable stock and mix. Let the mixture simmer for twenty minutes or till the broccoli is tender.
3. Remove the broccoli from the soup, cool and blend. Add it back to the soup and mix well. Cool and strain the mixture through a piece of muslin. Add the cream and reheat on medium heat for five minutes.
4. Remove the pan from heat, pour into individual soup bowls and serve hot, garnished with walnuts.

• **Preparation time:** 15-20 minutes • **Cooking time:** 40-45 minutes • **Serves:** 4

Tomato And Coriander Soup

Ingredients

5-6 medium tomatoes, chopped
½ teaspoon coriander seeds
4 teaspoons chopped fresh coriander
2 tablespoons butter
1 inch ginger, chopped
3-4 garlic cloves, chopped
1 tablespoon refined flour (*maida*)
4 bay leaves
Salt to taste
½ teaspoon white pepper powder
7½ cups vegetable stock

Method

1. Melt the butter in deep non-stick pan, add the coriander seeds and sauté till fragrant. Add the ginger and garlic and sauté for a minute.
2. Add the refined flour and cook till it turns just brown. Add the tomatoes and sauté for two to three minutes.
3. Add the bay leaves, salt, white pepper powder and vegetable stock and cook for twenty minutes on low heat.
4. Remove from heat and pass the soup through a soup strainer. Add half the chopped coriander and reheat till it comes to a boil.
5. Remove from heat and pour into individual soup bowls.
6. Serve hot, garnished with the remaining chopped coriander.

• **Preparation time:** 15-20 minutes • **Cooking time:** 40-45 minutes • **Serves:** 4

Mulligatawny Soup

Ingredients

500 grams boneless lamb, chopped finely
½ teaspoon turmeric powder
2 litres (10 cups) lamb white stock
5 teaspoons coriander powder
A pinch of fenugreek seeds (*methi dana*)
2 teaspoons cumin seeds
1 inch cinnamon
Salt to taste
A pinch of black pepper powder
2 inches ginger, chopped
4-5 garlic cloves, chopped
2 medium onions, sliced
2 sprigs curry leaves
4-5 medium tomatoes, chopped
½ cup coconut milk
4 teaspoons ghee
1 teaspoon lemon juice

Method

1. Place the lamb pieces in a deep non-stick pan. Add the turmeric powder and the stock and bring it to a boil. Reduce heat and cook till the lamb is tender.

2. Add the coriander powder, fenugreek seeds, cumin seeds and cinnamon. Divide the salt, pepper powder, ginger, garlic, onions, curry leaves and tomatoes in two portions and add one portion to the pan.

3. Let the mixture simmer for fifteen minutes or till the tomatoes soften. Remove from heat and remove the lamb pieces.

4. Pass the liquid through a soup strainer into another deep non-stick pan. Put the lamb pieces back in the soup. Add the coconut milk and stir.

5. Heat the ghee in a non-stick pan and sauté the remaining onions to a golden brown colour and add to the soup along with the lemon juice and the remaining salt, pepper powder, ginger, garlic, curry leaves and tomatoes. Increase heat and let the soup boil for five minutes.

6. Serve hot with boiled rice.

• **Preparation time:** 15-20 minutes • **Cooking time:** 1½ hrs • **Serves:** 4

Chicken Consommé

Ingredients

1 kg chicken on the bone
1 medium onion, halved
1 medium carrot, chopped
1 garlic clove
1 medium bunch (150 grams) fresh coriander leaves
1 bay leaf
3 eggs
Salt to taste

Method

1. Place the chicken, onion, carrot, garlic, coriander leaves, bay leaf and two litres water in a deep non-stick pan and bring to a boil on medium heat.
2. Reduce heat and simmer for one and a half to two hours. As the ingredients should ideally be always immersed in water, keep adding more water as and when required. Taste the stock after two hours and if it does not taste of chicken with a flavour of the vegetables, cook it for another thirty minutes.
3. Strain the stock through a large strainer and return stock to the pan. Simmer till it reduces to one litre. Remove from heat and allow the stock to cool before placing in the refrigerator for an hour. Skim off any fat from the surface.
4. Take few pieces of cooked chicken and cut into small cubes. Set aside for garnishing. Break the eggs and separate the yolks and add the whites to the stock and whisk thoroughly. Re-heat the stock to boiling point, whisking continuously.
5. After the stock starts boiling let it simmer for fifteen minutes until the egg whites form a crust on the surface. Line a sieve with a piece of clean, unused muslin that has been washed in plain water. (The use of detergent will affect the flavour of the consommé.)
6. Ladle the egg white crust into the sieve and then slowly ladle the liquid over the crust, allowing time for the stock to pass through the crust and the sieve before adding any more. The stock is not to be forced through the sieve.
7. Return the stock to the pan and re-heat but not to boiling point. The consommé should be served warm to hot, but not boiling, as it intensifies the flavour. Garnish with chicken cubes. If not serving immediately, cool the soup and refrigerate until required.

• **Preparation time:** 20-25 minutes • **Cooking time:** 2½ hours • **Serves:** 4

Bhindi Kurkuri

Ingredients

750 grams ladies' fingers (*okra/bhindi*)
Salt to taste
1 teaspoon red chilli powder
1 teaspoon *garam masala* powder
½ teaspoon dried mango powder (*amchur*)
3 tablespoons gram flour (*besan*)
Oil for deep-frying
2 inches ginger, cut into strips
2 green chillies, slit
½ teaspoon *chaat masala*

Method

1. Wipe each ladies' finger and trim both ends. Quarter them lengthways and spread them out on a flat dish. Sprinkle salt, chilli powder, *garam masala* powder and dried mango powder and mix well so that all the pieces are coated with the spices.
2. Sprinkle the gram flour over them and mix so they are coated evenly. Do not add water. Divide the ladies' finger pieces into two batches.
3. Heat sufficient oil in a *kadai* till it begins to smoke. Add half the ladies' finger pieces and deep-fry, keeping each piece separate with the help of a fork. Do not allow pieces to stick to each other.
4. Remove when the ladies' finger are crisp and brown in colour and drain on absorbent paper. Deep-fry the remaining ladies' finger pieces.
5. Serve hot, garnished with the ginger, green chillies and *chaat masala*.

• **Preparation time:** 20-25 minutes • **Cooking time:** 20-25 minutes • **Serves:** 4

Hara Kabab

Ingredients

1 kg shelled green peas, boiled
400 grams fresh spinach leaves, blanched and drained well
4 inches ginger, chopped
2 green chillies, chopped
2 tablespoons chopped fresh coriander
Salt to taste
½ teaspoon red chilli powder
½ teaspoon *garam masala* powder
1 teaspoon *chaat masala*
½ cup fresh breadcrumbs
¼ cup cornflour
Oil for deep-frying

Method

1. Mash the peas and place in a bowl. Purée the spinach without adding water and add to peas.
2. Add ginger, green chillies, chopped coriander, salt, chilli powder, *garam masala* powder, *chaat masala*, breadcrumbs and cornflour.
3. Divide into equal lemon-sized portions, roll them into balls and press them slightly to shape them into kababs.
4. Heat sufficient oil in a *kadai* and deep-fry the kababs, a few at a time, until they turn crisp and golden brown on both sides. Drain on absorbent paper.
5. Serve hot with Mint Chutney (refer page 117).

• **Preparation time:** 30-35 minutes • **Cooking time:** 20-25 minutes • **Serves:** 4

Dahi Bhalle

Ingredients

For bhalle

1 cup skinless split black gram (*dhuli urad dal*), soaked

Salt to taste

1 teaspoon cumin seeds

2 inches ginger, chopped

1 green chilli, chopped

Oil for deep-frying

For yogurt mixture

2 cups yogurt, whisked

2 teaspoons sugar

Salt to taste

¾ teaspoon roasted cumin powder

1 teaspoon black salt (*kala namak*)

1 teaspoon white pepper powder

For garnishing

1 inch ginger, cut into thin strips

2 green chillies, chopped

2 tablespoons chopped fresh coriander

2 teaspoons red chilli powder

2 teaspoons roasted cumin powder

2 tablespoons chopped fresh mint leaves

4 teaspoons sweet tamarind chutney

Method

1. Drain the split black gram and place in a blender jar. Grind to a smooth paste, using little water as required. Transfer to a bowl, add the salt, cumin seeds, ginger and green chillies and mix well. Whisk vigorously in order to make the batter light.
2. Heat sufficient oil in a *kadai*; collect and pick up a small portion of the batter using your fingertips and drop small *bhalle* into the oil. Deep-fry till they turn golden. Drain and soak in lukewarm water to soften.
3. Mix together the yogurt, sugar, salt, cumin powder, black salt and white pepper powder in a bowl.
4. Remove the *bhalle* from water, squeeze gently to drain out water and add them to the yogurt. Let them soak for ten to fifteen minutes. Keep in the refrigerator to chill.
5. Serve the *bhalle*, garnished with the ginger strips, green chillies, chopped coriander, chilli powder, roasted cumin powder, mint leaves and sweet tamarind chutney.

• **Preparation time:** 2 hours • **Cooking time:** 30-35 minutes • **Serves:** 4

Jhinga Til Tikka

Ingredients

16 large prawns (*jhinga*), shelled and deveined

2 tablespoons roasted skinless split black gram (*dhuli urad dal*)

3½ tablespoons white sesame seeds (*safed til*)

Oil for deep-frying

First marinade

2 tablespoons ginger paste

2 tablespoons garlic paste

½ teaspoon white pepper powder

½ teaspoon red chilli powder

Salt to taste

4 tablespoons lemon juice

Second marinade

4 tablespoons grated cheese

½ cup drained (hung) yogurt

1½ teaspoons carom seeds (*ajwain*)

¼ cup fresh cream

½ teaspoon mace (*javitri*) powder

⅓ teaspoon green cardamom powder

4 eggs

To serve

1 medium onion, cut into rings

1 lemon, cut into wedges

Mint Chutney (refer page 117), as required

Method

1. For the first marinade, mix together the ginger paste, garlic paste, white pepper powder, chilli powder, salt and lemon juice. Add the prawns and mix well and marinate for thirty minutes.
2. For the second marinade, mix together the cheese, yogurt, carom seeds, cream, mace powder, cardamom powder and eggs. Add the prawns and mix well and marinate for thirty minutes.
3. Grind the split black gram to a powder and combine with sesame seeds in a bowl.
4. Heat sufficient oil in a *kadai*. Lightly dust the prawns with the black gram-sesame mixture and deep-fry in hot oil till the prawns turn golden. Drain on absorbent paper. Alternatively, brush the marinated prawns with oil and roast in a gas *tandoor*.
5. Serve hot with onion rings, lemon wedges and mint chutney.

• **Preparation time:** 1 hour • **Cooking time:** 15-20 minutes • **Serves:** 4

Tandoori Prawns

Ingredients

12 (30 grams each approx.) jumbo prawns

Butter, as required

First marinade

8 teaspoons lemon juice

2 teaspoons ginger paste

2 teaspoons garlic paste

½ teaspoon red chilli powder

Salt to taste

Second marinade

1 cup yogurt

½ cup fresh cream

4 teaspoons lemon juice

2 tablespoons ginger paste

2 tablespoons garlic paste

1 teaspoon onion seeds (*kalonji*)

A pinch turmeric powder

A pinch nutmeg powder (*jaiphal*)

A pinch mace powder (*javitri*)

A pinch green cardamom powder

1 teaspoon black pepper powder

Salt to taste

To serve

1 medium onion, cut into rings

1 lemon, cut into wedges

Mint Chutney (refer page 117), as required

Method

1. Shell the prawns, retaining the tails. Devein, wash well and pat them dry on an absorbent paper carefully and place them in a bowl. For the first marinade, mix together the lemon juice, ginger paste, garlic paste, chilli powder and salt and rub it on the prawns and marinate for fifteen minutes.
2. For the second marinade, whisk together the yogurt, cream, lemon juice, ginger paste, garlic paste, onion seeds, turmeric powder, nutmeg powder, mace powder, cardamom powder, pepper powder and salt and rub it on the prawns.
3. Marinate in the refrigerator for thirty minutes. Thread the prawns onto skewers and set aside for five to ten minutes to allow juices to drain off.
4. Roast the prawns in a *tandoor* or pre-heated oven at 170°C/325°F/Gas Mark 3 for two to three minutes. Alternatively, you can cook the prawns in a gas *tandoor*.
5. Remove from *tandoor*/oven and hang the skewers to allow juices to drain off. Baste the prawns with butter and roast again for three to four minutes. Remove the prawns from the skewers and serve hot, garnished with the onion rings and lemon wedges and fresh mint chutney.

• **Preparation time:** 1½ hours • **Cooking time:** 10-15 minutes • **Serves:** 4

Jalpari Kabab

Ingredients

12 thin fillets of sole (*repti/morrul*)
12 medium prawns, shelled

First marinade

5 teaspoons ginger-garlic paste
5 teaspoons mango pickle *masala*
⅓ teaspoon onion seeds (*kalonji*)
1 teaspoon white pepper powder
¾ teaspoon *garam masala* powder
Salt to taste
1 teaspoon red chilli powder
1 teaspoon lemon juice
4 teaspoons oil

Second marinade

¾ cup yogurt
6 teaspoons fresh cream
A few strands of saffron (*kesar*)
A pinch of green cardamom powder

Method

1. Pat dry the fish fillets and prawns.
2. For the first marinade, place the ginger-garlic paste in a piece of muslin and squeeze to extract juice into a bowl. Add the pickle *masala*, onion seeds, white pepper powder, *garam masala* powder, salt, chilli powder, lemon juice and oil and mix well.
3. Use half of this marinade to rub onto the fillets and set aside for five minutes.
4. For the second marinade mix yogurt, cream, saffron and cardamom powder and mix in the remaining first marinade. Set aside.
5. Put each fillet flat on a table top. Place a prawn at one end of the fillet and roll up the fillet around the prawn. The tail end of the prawn should be visible. Wrap each fillet roll tightly with cling wrap or aluminium foil.
6. Boil five cups of water in a deep non-stick pan, slide in the fillet rolls, cover and cook for ten minutes. Drain the water and place rolls under running water for one minute. Remove the wrap/foil and marinate rolls in the second marinade for five minutes.
7. Thread the rolls onto skewers and roast in *tandoor* or oven (170°C/325°F/Gas Mark 3) for ten minutes. Remove the rolls from skewers, transfer to a serving plate. Serve hot with Mint Chutney (refer page 117).

• **Preparation time:** 40-45 minutes • **Cooking time:** 20-25 minutes • **Serves:** 4

Galouti Kabab

Ingredients

800 grams minced lamb (*keema*)
4 teaspoons ginger-garlic paste
4 teaspoons unripe green papaya paste
1 teaspoon red chilli powder
½ teaspoon mace powder (*javitri*)
½ teaspoon *garam masala* powder
Salt to taste
2 teaspoons butter
4 teaspoons gram flour (*besan*)
Ghee for deep-frying

To serve

1 medium onion, cut into rings
1 lemon, cut into wedges
Mint Chutney (refer page 117), as required

Method

1. Blend the minced lamb with ginger-garlic paste, papaya paste, chilli powder, mace powder, *garam masala* powder, salt, butter and gram flour. Keep it in a refrigerator for two to three hours to marinate.
2. Divide the mixture into equal portions and shape them into patties (kababs).
3. Heat sufficient ghee in a *kadai* and deep-fry the kababs till they turn golden all around. Drain on absorbent paper.
4. Serve hot with onion rings, lemon wedges and mint chutney.

• **Preparation time:** 15-20 minutes • **Cooking time:** 35-40 minutes • **Serves:** 4

Murgh Daraanpur

Ingredients

8 (100 grams each approx.) boneless chicken breasts

Oil for deep-frying

For paste

¾ teaspoon red chilli powder

⅓ teaspoon *garam masala* powder

A pinch of powdered dried fenugreek leaves (*kasoori methi*)

A pinch of white pepper powder

Salt to taste

3 teaspoons ginger-garlic paste

1 teaspoon vinegar

1 teaspoon oil

For filling

10 pieces marinated chicken *tikka*

3 cups grated cheese

4 tablespoons raisins (*kishmish*), chopped

8-10 cashew nuts

2⅓ teaspoons chopped fresh coriander

2-3 green chillies, chopped

For batter

½ cup cornflour

1 teaspoon vinegar

A pinch of salt

A pinch of red chilli powder

4 tablespoons refined flour (*maida*)

1 teaspoon ginger paste

1 teaspoon garlic paste

2 eggs, whisked

Method

1. Pat the chicken breasts dry.
2. For the paste, mix together chilli powder, *garam masala* powder, dried fenugreek leaves, white pepper powder, salt, ginger-garlic paste, vinegar and oil.
3. Slit the chicken breasts from the sides, open out and flatten with a mallet without tearing the flesh. Apply the prepared paste on chicken breasts evenly.
4. To prepare the filling, grill the chicken *tikka*; chop them into small pieces and put into a bowl. Add the cheese, raisins, cashew nuts, chopped coriander and green chillies. Mix well.
5. Divide the filling into eight equal portions and place in the centre of each breast piece. Roll the pieces firmly over the filling and refrigerate for ten minutes.

6. Whisk the cornflour with one and half cups water to make a smooth batter with no lumps. Add the vinegar, salt, chilli powder, refined flour, ginger paste, garlic paste and whisked eggs and whisk again.
7. Heat sufficient oil in a *kadai*, dip each rolled-up chicken piece in the batter and deep-fry on medium heat till half done. Drain on absorbent paper.
8. Deep-fry the chicken pieces again till golden brown. Drain them again on absorbent paper. Cut each piece into half and serve with the onion slices and lemon wedges.

• **Preparation time:** 1 hour • **Cooking time:** 35-40 minutes • **Serves:** 4

Tandoori Chicken

Ingredients

800 grams chicken on the bone
Oil for basting

For marinade

½ cup yogurt
4 teaspoons ginger-garlic paste
1 teaspoon *garam masala* powder
Salt to taste
1 teaspoon red chilli powder

To serve

1 lemon, cut into wedges
1 medium onion, cut into rings
Mint Chutney (refer page 117), as required

Method

1. The chicken can be used whole or cut into four pieces. Make deep cuts in the flesh with a knife.
2. To prepare the marinade, mix together the yogurt, garlic-ginger paste, *garam masala* powder, salt and chilli powder. Rub the marinade onto the chicken pieces and keep them in a refrigerator for four to five hours to marinate.
3. Grill the chicken pieces in a *tandoor* or over a charcoal fire, basting with oil two to three times, till the chicken is completely cooked and golden brown on the outside.
4. Place them on a serving platter and serve with lemon wedges, onion rings and fresh mint chutney.

• **Preparation time:** 30-35 minutes • **Cooking time:** 40-45 minutes • **Serves:** 4

Tangri Kabab

Ingredients

12 chicken drumsticks
Oil for basting
3 tablespoons cashew nut powder
4 eggs, whisked

First marinade

4 teaspoons ginger-garlic paste
A pinch white pepper powder
Salt to taste
1 teaspoon vinegar

Second marinade

1⅓ cups yogurt
⅔ cup fresh cream
1 tablespoon ginger paste
1 tablespoon garlic paste
⅓ teaspoon white pepper powder
¾ teaspoon *garam masala* powder
Salt to taste
A few strands of saffron (*kesar*)

To serve

1 medium onion, cut into rings
1 lemon, cut into wedges

Method

1. Make four to five vertical cuts on the chicken drumsticks.
2. For the first marinade, mix together the ginger-garlic paste, white pepper powder, salt and vinegar and coat the drumsticks with it and rub into the cuts. Marinate for fifteen minutes in a refrigerator.
3. For the second marinade, mix together the yogurt, cream, ginger paste, garlic paste, white pepper powder, *garam masala* powder, salt and saffron.
4. Apply the marinade on the drumsticks and marinate for fifteen minutes in a refrigerator. Thread the drumsticks onto skewers; brush with oil and roast in *tandoor* or gas oven for three to five minutes or till half cooked.
5. Remove and let it rest for two to three minutes. Baste with oil and roast till completely cooked. Mix the cashew nut powder and eggs and coat the drumsticks with this mixture and roast again till the egg coating cooks.
6. Remove from *tandoor* and serve hot with onion rings and lemon wedges.

• **Preparation time:** 1 hour • **Cooking time:** 25-30 minutes • **Serves:** 4

Seekh Kabab

Ingredients

500 grams minced lamb (*keema*)

2 teaspoons unripe green papaya paste

Salt to taste

1 teaspoon red chilli powder

½ teaspoon caraway seeds (*shahi jeera*)

½ teaspoon nutmeg powder (*jaiphal*)

1 teaspoon dried fenugreek leaves (*kasoori methi*)

2 teaspoons cornflour

1 teaspoon poppy seed powder (*khus khus*)

2 teaspoons cashew nut paste

½ teaspoon ginger-garlic paste

1 small onion, minced

3-4 green chillies, chopped

1 medium bunch (100 grams) fresh coriander, chopped

½ teaspoon *garam masala* powder

1 egg

Oil for basting

To serve

1 medium onion, cut into rings

1 lemon, cut into wedges

Mint Chutney (refer page 117), as required

Method

1. Mix the mince with unripe papaya paste and marinate for half an hour.
2. Combine together the salt, chilli powder, caraway seeds, nutmeg, dried fenugreek leaves, cornflour, poppy seed powder, cashew nut paste, ginger-garlic paste, onion, green chillies, chopped coriander and *garam masala* powder and grind to a paste.
3. Add the egg and mix the paste with the mince. Divide the mixture into twelve equal portions. Moisten the hands and press each portion onto a skewer (*seekh*), four-inch in length and one-fourth-inch thick.
4. Grill the *seekh* kababs on charcoal fire. Baste the kababs with oil while grilling. Cook till browned from all sides before sliding them off the skewers.
5. Serve hot with the onion slices, lemon wedges and fresh mint chutney.

• **Preparation time:** 45-45 minutes • **Cooking time:** 1 hour • **Serves:** 4

Kallan Kabab

Ingredients

For lamb kabab

250 grams minced lamb (*keema*)

125 grams lamb kidney (*gurda*)

125 grams lamb liver (*kaleji*)

Salt to taste

¾ teaspoon red chilli powder

⅓ teaspoon *garam masala* powder

A pinch of powdered dried fenugreek leaves (*kasoori methi*)

2 teaspoons ginger-garlic paste

2 tablespoons chopped fresh coriander

2 green chillies, chopped

For chicken coating

500 grams minced chicken

Salt to taste

½ teaspoon white pepper powder

A pinch *garam masala* powder

A pinch of powdered dried fenugreek leaves (*kasoori methi*)

⅓ teaspoon ginger-garlic paste

¾ teaspoon chopped fresh coriander

4 teaspoons butter

To serve

1 medium onion, cut into rings

1 lemon, cut into wedges

Mint Chutney (refer page 117), as required

Method

1. Blend together the minced lamb, kidney, liver, salt, chilli powder, *garam masala* powder, dried fenugreek leaves, ginger-garlic paste, chopped coriander and green chillies and process till smooth. Set aside for fifteen minutes.

2. Pat the mince mixture on to skewers and roast in charcoal grill for eight to ten minutes. Remove from the grill, place the skewers upright to allow excess juices to drain off. Set the skewers aside for three to five minutes. Retain the kababs on the skewers.

3. Meanwhile, for the chicken coating, mix minced chicken, salt, white pepper powder, *garam masala* powder, dried fenugreek leaves, ginger-garlic paste and chopped coriander. Coat the minced lamb kababs evenly with the minced chicken mixture and roast in the grill for five to six minutes.

4. Baste the kababs with butter and remove them from skewers. Serve hot, with the onion rings, lemon wedges and mint chutney.

• **Preparation time:** 1 hour • **Cooking time:** 40-45 minutes • **Serves:** 4

Main Dishes
Vegetarian

Palm Court

होटल कनिष्क
Hotel Kanishka

Gatte Ki Sabzi

Ingredients

2 cups gram flour (*besan*)
2 teaspoons red chilli powder
4 teaspoons coriander powder
Salt to taste
2 tablespoons ghee
1½ cups drained (hung) yogurt
A pinch turmeric powder
4 tablespoons oil
2 teaspoons cumin seeds

Method

1. Mix the gram flour, one teaspoon chilli powder, one teaspoon coriander powder, salt and ghee. Add sufficient water and knead into a stiff dough. Divide into twelve equal portions and shape them into one-inch thick rolls.
2. Heat sufficient water in a deep non-stick pan, add the dough rolls and boil till they are cooked. Drain, cool and cut into one-inch pieces. Reserve the cooking liquid.
3. Mix the yogurt, remaining chilli powder, remaining coriander powder, turmeric powder and salt in a large bowl. Add the cooked pieces of dough (*gatte*).
4. Heat oil in a non-stick pan. Add the cumin seeds and when they begin to change colour, add the yogurt-*gatte* mixture.
5. Cook on high heat till the mixture comes to a boil. Reduce heat and let the mixture simmer on low heat for five minutes. If need be, adjust the consistency using a little of the cooking liquid.
6. Transfer the *gatte ki sabzi* into a serving bowl. Serve with rice or *roti*.

• **Preparation time:** 20-25 minutes • **Cooking time:** 40-45 minutes • **Serves:** 4

Dal Baati

Ingredients

For baati

2 cups refined flour (*maida*)

½ cup semolina (*sooji/rawa*)

Salt to taste

¾ cup ghee

For dal

1 cup split red lentils (*masoor dal*), soaked

¼ cup oil

2 teaspoons cumin seeds

3 green chillies, chopped

6-8 garlic cloves, chopped

1 tablespoon red chilli powder

2 teaspoons *garam masala* powder

1 medium tomato, chopped

Method

1. Preheat oven to 180°C/350°F/Gas Mark 4.
2. For making the *baati*, mix the flour, semolina, salt and half a cup ghee in a bowl and knead into a dough using water as needed.
3. Divide the dough into small equal portions and roll into balls and arrange them on a baking tray.
4. Bake them in the preheated oven till they turn brown. Apply a little ghee on each ball. The *baati* are ready.
5. Drain and boil the lentil with four cups of water in a deep non-stick pan till done.
6. Heat the oil in another non-stick pan and add the cumin seeds, green chillies, garlic, chilli powder, *garam masala* powder and tomato and sauté till fragrant.
7. Add the boiled *dal* with the water and mix. Cover the pan and let it simmer on medium heat for five minutes. The *dal* is ready.
8. Serve *dal* and *baati* drizzled with ghee.

• **Preparation time:** 20-25 minutes • **Cooking time:** 40-45 minutes • **Serves:** 4

Chhole

Ingredients

1½ cups chickpeas (*kabuli chana*), soaked overnight

2 inches ginger, chopped

6-7 garlic cloves, crushed

¼ cup oil

1 teaspoon cumin seeds

3 green chillies, slit

1½ teaspoon red chilli powder

Salt to taste

2 teaspoons ginger-garlic paste

1 teaspoon coriander powder

1 teaspoon cumin powder

1 teaspoon dried mango powder (*amchur*)

½ teaspoon *garam masala* powder

1 teaspoon powdered dried pomegranate seeds (*anardana)*

¼ cup tomato purée

For garnishing

2 teaspoons chopped fresh coriander

1 medium onion, cut into rings

1 lemon, sliced

Method

1. Drain and pressure-cook the chickpeas with three cups of water, ginger and garlic till pressure is released four to five times (four to five whistles) or till the chickpeas are completely soft. Open the lid when the pressure has reduced completely. Strain and reserve the cooking liquid.

2. Heat the oil in a non-stick pan, add the cumin seeds, green chillies and half teaspoon chilli powder and sauté till fragrant.

3. Add the boiled chickpeas along with the cooking liquid and salt. Cover the pan and cook over medium heat till all the water evaporates.

4. Add the ginger-garlic paste, coriander powder, cumin powder, remaining chilli powder, dried mango powder, *garam masala* powder and powdered dried pomegranate seeds and sauté for four to five minutes.

5. Add the tomato purée and when the mixture comes to a boil lower the heat and cook for three to four minutes.

6. Transfer the *chhole* into a serving bowl. Garnish with the chopped coriander, onion rings and lemon slices. Serve hot with *naan* or Bhature (refer page 110).

• **Preparation time:** 25-30 minutes • **Cooking time:** 35-40 minutes • **Serves:** 4

Bhagare Baingan

Ingredients

500 grams small round brinjal (*baingan*)
2 tablespoons oil
4 teaspoons white sesame seeds (*safed til*)
4 teaspoons peanuts
4 teaspoons freshly grated coconut
1 teaspoon ginger-garlic paste
2 medium onions, chopped
½ teaspoon turmeric powder
½ teaspoon *garam masala* powder
½ teaspoon cumin powder
½ teaspoon coriander powder
Red chilli powder to taste
Salt to taste
2 teaspoons tamarind pulp
4 teaspoons chopped fresh coriander

Method

1. Slit the brinjal from both ends, without cutting through.
2. Heat one and a half tablespoons of oil in a non-stick pan and sauté the brinjal till they become soft. Drain and set aside.
3. Dry-roast the sesame seeds and peanuts till fragrant. Grind them with the coconut to a smooth paste. Set aside.
4. Add the remaining oil to the same pan, add the ginger-garlic paste and onions and sauté on medium heat till onions turn light brown.
5. Add the sesame-peanuts-coconut paste and sauté for a minute. Add the turmeric powder, *garam masala* powder, cumin powder, coriander powder and chilli powder. Mix well.
6. Add the salt and tamarind pulp and mix well. Add the fried brinjals, cover and cook till the brinjal are done.
7. Garnish with the chopped coriander and serve hot.

• **Preparation time:** 45-50 minutes • **Cooking time:** 25-30 minutes • **Serves:** 4

Baingan Ka Bharta

Ingredients

500 grams large brinjals (*baingan*)
¼ cup oil
2 teaspoons cumin seeds
4 medium onions, chopped
2 tablespoons ginger-garlic paste
2 medium tomatoes, chopped
1 teaspoon coriander powder
1 teaspoon cumin powder
1 teaspoon *garam masala* powder
3 green chillies, chopped
Salt to taste
4 tablespoons chopped fresh coriander

Method

1. Roast the brinjal on direct flame till the skin gets charred and the inner flesh softens.
2. Cool the brinjal, remove the charred skin, mash the inner flesh coarsely in a plate. Set aside.
3. Heat the oil in a non-stick pan, add the cumin seeds and sauté till they change colour. Add the onions and sauté till they turn translucent. Add the ginger-garlic paste and sauté for one minute.
4. Add the tomatoes, coriander powder, cumin powder and *garam masala* powder. Stir well and sauté for three to five minutes, stirring frequently. Sprinkle water to prevent the spices from scorching.
5. Add the roasted brinjal and mix well. Add the green chillies, salt and chopped coriander, stir and cook for another minute. Serve hot with bread or rice.

Chef's Tip

You can roast the brinjals in an oven, on a gas stove burner, on a barbecue or in a tandoor.

• **Preparation time:** 30-35 minutes • **Cooking time:** 25-30 minutes • **Serves:** 4

Palak Paneer

Ingredients

500 grams fresh spinach leaves

500 grams cottage cheese (*paneer*), cubed

2 tablespoons oil

1 teaspoon cumin seeds

3 bay leaves

1 inch ginger, chopped

4-5 garlic cloves, chopped

4 medium onions, grated

2-3 medium tomatoes, chopped

Salt to taste

1 teaspoon *garam masala* powder

2 teaspoons red chilli powder

Method

1. Trim the spinach leaves and blanch them. Drain, cool and make a purée.
2. Heat the oil in a non-stick pan; add the cumin seeds. When the seeds change colour, add the bay leaves, ginger and garlic. Sauté till mixture is light brown.
3. Add the onions and sauté till golden brown. Add the tomatoes and cook on medium heat till the oil begins to separate. Add the salt, *garam masala* powder and chilli powder. Stir till well mixed.
4. Add the puréed spinach and sauté for two to three minutes before adding the cottage cheese.
5. Mix well and serve hot with *roti*.

• **Preparation time:** 20-25 minutes • **Cooking time:** 30-35 minutes • **Serves:** 4

Paneer Kofta

Ingredients

500 grams cottage cheese (*paneer*)
1 teaspoon arrowroot powder
½ cup chopped fresh coriander + for garnishing
Salt to taste
3 tablespoons oil + for deep-frying
½ teaspoon cumin seeds
1 teaspoon turmeric powder
1 tablespoon coriander powder
1 teaspoon red chilli powder
1 teaspoon *garam masala* powder
¼ cup onion paste
¼ cup yogurt, whisked

Method

1. Mash the cottage cheese in a bowl; add the arrowroot powder, chopped coriander and salt. Mix well.
2. Divide into small equal portions and roll into balls of one-inch diameter.
3. Heat sufficient oil in a *kadai* and deep-fry the balls till light golden brown. Drain on absorbent paper. Set aside.
4. Heat three tablespoons oil in a non-stick pan, add the cumin seeds, turmeric powder, coriander powder, chilli powder, *garam masala* powder, onion paste and salt. Sauté till the oil separates.
5. Add the yogurt and half a cup of water and mix well. Let the mixture simmer till it gets a creamy consistency.
6. Add the *kofta* and mix gently.
7. Serve hot, garnished with chopped coriander.

• **Preparation time:** 15-20 minutes • **Cooking time:** 30-35 minutes • **Serves:** 4

Paneer Pasanda

Ingredients

600 grams cottage cheese (*paneer*) block

Oil for deep-frying

For filling

¼ cup grated cottage cheese (*paneer*)

2 teaspoons chopped cashew nuts

1 teaspoon pickle *masala*

4 teaspoons tomato purée

For batter

⅛ cup cornflour

Salt to taste

For gravy

2 teaspoons oil

2 teaspoons ginger-garlic paste

2 cups tomato purée

Salt to taste

½ teaspoon red chilli powder

A pinch of white pepper powder

A pinch of powdered dried fenugreek leaves (*kasoori methi*)

2 teaspoons *garam masala* powder

2 teaspoons butter

4 teaspoons fresh cream + for garnishing

Method

1. Cut the cottage cheese into sixteen finger-shaped pieces.
2. For the filling, mix together the cottage cheese, cashew nuts, pickle *masala* and tomato purée. Stuff the filling in between two cottage cheese fingers like a sandwich.
3. For the batter, beat together cornflour, salt and one cup water till smooth. Heat sufficient oil in a *kadai*. Dip the cottage cheese sandwiches in the batter and deep-fry for two to three minutes. Drain on absorbent paper.
4. For the gravy, heat the oil in a non-stick pan, add the ginger-garlic paste and sauté for two to three minutes.
5. Add the tomato purée and cook for eight to ten minutes or till the purée thickens. Add the salt, chilli powder, white pepper powder, powdered dried fenugreek leaves and *garam masala* powder and mix well.
6. Cook for three to five minutes, stir in the butter and cream. Remove the pan from heat. Arrange the fried cottage cheese sandwiches on a serving dish and pour the gravy on top. Garnish with a little cream and serve hot.

• **Preparation time:** 20-25 minutes • **Cooking time:** 35-40 minutes • **Serves:** 4

Lauki Nazakat

Ingredients

400 grams bottle gourd (*lauki/doodhi*)
100 grams cottage cheese (*paneer*)
10-15 cashew nuts, chopped
2 tablespoons melon seeds (*magaz*)
10-12 raisins (*kishmish*)
Salt to taste
1 teaspoon red chilli powder
½ teaspoon *garam masala* powder
½ cup whole-wheat flour (*atta*)
Oil for deep-frying

For gravy
¼ cup oil
7-8 cloves
5-6 green cardamoms
1 black cardamom
1 teaspoon cinnamon powder
4 bay leaves
2 tablespoons ginger-garlic paste
½ cup cashew nut paste
½ cup yogurt
½ cup browned onion paste
1 cup tomato purée
Salt to taste
2 teaspoons coriander powder
1 teaspoon red chilli powder
½ teaspoon white pepper powder
½ cup fresh cream
2-3 drops screw pine essence (*kewda jal*)

Method

1. Peel and cut the two ends of the bottle gourd and scoop out the centre to make a hollow tube.
2. For the filling, mix together the cottage cheese, cashew nuts, melon seeds, raisins, salt, chilli powder and *garam masala* powder. Stuff the bottle gourd with the filling.
3. Make a paste of the flour with sufficient water and seal both ends of the bottle gourd with the paste.
4. Heat sufficient oil in a *kadai* and deep-fry the stuffed bottle gourd. Do not allow the colour of the bottle gourd to change. Drain on absorbent paper.
5. For the gravy, heat the oil in a non-stick pan; add the cloves, cardamoms, black cardamom, cinnamon powder and bay leaves and sauté till fragrant. Add the ginger-garlic paste mixed with a little water and sauté for a minute.
6. Mix the cashew nut paste in yogurt and add. Mix and cook for five to ten minutes. Add the browned onion paste, tomato purée, salt, coriander powder, chilli powder

and white pepper powder. Cover and cook on low heat, stirring continuously till the gravy thickens. Remove the pan from heat.

7. Stir in the cream and *kewda jal*. Remove the bay leaves from the gravy. Cut the fried bottle gourd into one-and-half-inch thick slices and arrange them on a serving dish, with each slice slightly overlapping the other.

8. Pour the curry on top of the slices. Serve hot with any Indian bread.

• **Preparation time:** 1 hour • **Cooking time:** 25-30 minutes • **Serves:** 4

Haaq

Ingredients

1 kg Kashmiri spinach (*haaq*)
2 tablespoons mustard oil
1 teaspoon mustard seeds
2 cups sliced leeks
Salt to taste
A pinch of *garam masala* powder

Method

1. Remove the tough stalks from the Kashmiri spinach and wash the leaves well.
2. Heat the mustard oil in a non-stick pan till it begins to smoke. Allow to cool a little and place the pan back on heat.
3. Add the mustard seeds, leeks, salt and *garam masala* powder and sauté till the seeds splutter.
4. Add the spinach and cook till the leaves wilt.
5. Add one cup of water and cook, uncovered, on medium heat for ten to fifteen minutes or till most of the water evaporates.
6. Serve hot with rice.

• **Preparation time:** 10-15 minutes • **Cooking time:** 15-20 minutes • **Serves:** 4

Nadru Yakhni

Ingredients

450 grams lotus stems (*nadru/ bhein/kamal kakdi*)

Mustard oil for deep-frying

3-4 cloves

3 green cardamoms

1 tablespoon fennel (*saunf*) powder

½ teaspoon cinnamon powder

½ teaspoon cumin powder

2 black cardamoms

Salt to taste

3 cups yogurt, whisked

Method

1. Scrape away the skin of lotus stems. Trim the ends and cut into half-inch thick slices. Wash well and drain.
2. Heat sufficient mustard oil in a *kadai* till smoking point. Allow it to cool slightly and then place on the heat again. Slide in the lotus stem slices and deep-fry till half cooked. Drain on absorbent paper.
3. Place the lotus stems in a non-stick pan, add one cup of water and bring to a boil. Add the cloves, cardamoms, fennel powder, cinnamon powder, cumin powder, black cardamoms and salt. Stir well.
4. Boil on medium heat till the water is reduced to half its original quantity.
5. Stir in the yogurt, cover and cook, stirring occasionally, till the curry is well blended and the lotus stems are tender.
6. Remove from heat, transfer into a serving dish and serve hot.

• **Preparation time:** 20-25 minutes • **Cooking time:** 40-45 minutes • **Serves:** 4

Gobhi Mussallam

Ingredients

500 grams cauliflower, separated into florets
A pinch of turmeric powder
Salt to taste
4 bay leaves
2 tablespoons oil
7-8 cloves
5-6 green cardamoms
2 teaspoons ginger-garlic paste
1 tablespoon butter
A pinch of *garam masala* powder
2 teaspoons red chilli powder
A pinch of white pepper powder
4 tablespoons cashew nut paste
4 tablespoons yogurt
¼ cup tomato purée
¼ cup browned onion paste
2 tablespoons cream

Method

1. Boil sufficient water in a deep non-stick pan; add the turmeric powder, salt and bay leaves. Add the cauliflower florets, cover and cook on medium heat till the florets are three-fourth done.
2. Preheat oven to 200°C/400°F/Gas Mark 6.
3. Drain and transfer the cauliflower florets into an ovenproof bowl. Set aside. Heat the oil in another non-stick pan; add the cloves and green cardamoms and sauté till fragrant.
4. Add the ginger-garlic paste mixed with a teaspoon of water. When the water evaporates; add the butter, *garam masala* powder, chilli powder and white pepper powder and mix.
5. Mix the cashew nut paste and yogurt with half a cup of water and add to the pan. Cook on low heat till the mixture comes to a boil.
6. Stir in the tomato purée and browned onion paste. Cover and cook for five minutes. Remove the pan from heat and stir in the cream. Pour the contents over the cauliflower in the bowl.
7. Bake the *gobhi mussallam* in the preheated oven for five to ten minutes. Remove the bowl from the oven, transfer the contents into a serving bowl and serve hot.

• **Preparation time:** 10-15 minutes • **Cooking time:** 30-35 minutes • **Serves:** 4

Potato Curry

Ingredients

6 medium potatoes
1 teaspoon coriander powder
1 teaspoon turmeric powder
½ teaspoon *garam masala* powder
½ teaspoon asafoetida
2 teaspoons red chilli powder
2 teaspoons oil
2 teaspoons cumin seeds
2 teaspoons mustard seeds
2 inches ginger, chopped
4-5 garlic cloves, grated
1 green chilli, chopped
2 sprigs curry leaves
1 cup yogurt, whisked
Salt to taste
¼ teaspoon whole-wheat flour (*atta*)
2 teaspoons chopped fresh coriander

Method

1. Boil, peel and slice the potatoes. Mash half of them and set aside.
2. Mix the coriander powder, turmeric powder, *garam masala* powder, asafoetida and chilli powder in a quarter cup of water and set aside.
3. Heat the oil in a non-stick pan. Add the cumin seeds and mustard seeds and when they splutter, add the ginger, garlic, green chillies and curry leaves and sauté for two minutes.
4. Add the spice mixture and one cup of water and mix well. Cook for two minutes.
5. Add the yogurt and sauté till the yogurt loses its whiteness.
6. Add three-fourth cup of water, mashed potatoes, salt and flour. Stir well. Add the sliced potatoes.
7. When the mixture comes to a boil, lower the heat and let it cook for ten minutes or till the gravy thickens.
8. Garnish with the chopped coriander and serve hot with rice.

• **Preparation time:** 15-20 minutes • **Cooking time:** 15-20 minutes • **Serves:** 4

Sarson Ka Saag

Ingredients

1 kg fresh mustard leaves (*sarson*), chopped

250 grams fresh spinach leaves (*palak*), chopped

Salt to taste

3 green chillies, chopped

¼ cup ghee

2-3 medium onions, chopped

2 tablespoons ginger-garlic paste

1 teaspoon *garam masala* powder

2 teaspoons cornmeal (*makai ka atta*)

White unsalted butter, for garnishing

For seasoning

1 tablespoon ghee

1 inch ginger, chopped

1 green chilli, chopped

1 teaspoon red chilli powder

Method

1. Heat one cup of water in a deep non-stick pan; add the mustard leaves and spinach, a pinch of salt and the green chillies and cook, uncovered, on medium heat, for fifteen to twenty minutes or till completely cooked.
2. Drain the leaves and grind to a coarse paste.
3. Heat the ghee in a non-stick pan, add the onions and sauté till browned. Add the ginger-garlic paste, *garam masala* powder and cornmeal. Stir well and add the ground leaves and mix well.
4. For the seasoning, heat the ghee in a small non-stick pan, add the ginger, green chilli and chilli powder and sauté for half a minute. Add to the hot *saag* and mix lightly. Stir well and cook on low heat till the ghee separates.
5. Transfer into a serving dish, drop a dollop of white unsalted butter over it and serve hot with *makki di roti*.

• **Preparation time:** 20-25 minutes • **Cooking time:** 30-35 minutes • **Serves:** 4

Roghni Mushrooms

Ingredients

600 grams fresh button mushrooms, stalks removed
2 tablespoons oil
4 bay leaves
⅓ teaspoon mace (*javitri*) powder
7-8 cloves
5-6 green cardamoms
2 black cardamoms
1 teaspoon cinnamon powder
4 teaspoons ginger-garlic paste
1 cup tomato purée
Salt to taste
2 teaspoons red chilli powder
1 teaspoon turmeric powder
2 teaspoons coriander powder
¾ cup browned onion paste
¼ cup yogurt, whisked
A pinch of *garam masala* powder
2 tablespoons chopped fresh coriander
1 inch ginger, cut into thin strips
1 green chilli, chopped

Method

1. Heat the oil in a non-stick pan; add the bay leaves, mace, cloves, cardamoms and cinnamon powder and sauté till fragrant.

2. Add the ginger-garlic paste mixed with a little water and sauté till the water evaporates. Add the tomato purée, salt, chilli powder, turmeric powder and coriander powder and sauté for two to three minutes or till the oil separates.

3. Add the browned onion paste and yogurt, sauté for two to three minutes. Add the mushrooms and, half cup of water, mix well and cook on low heat till the curry thickens. Remove the pan from heat and transfer into a serving dish.

4. Sprinkle *garam masala* powder and serve hot garnished with the chopped coriander, ginger strips and green chilli.

• **Preparation time:** 40-45 minutes • **Cooking time:** 30-35 minutes • **Serves:** 4

Shabnam Curry

Ingredients

250 grams fresh button mushrooms
2 medium potatoes, boiled and peeled
4 tablespoons oil
1 medium onion, chopped
1 medium tomato, chopped
3 teaspoons ginger-garlic paste
Salt to taste
1 teaspoon coriander powder
1 teaspoon red chilli powder
1 teaspoon turmeric powder
½ cup boiled green peas
5 teaspoons cashew nut paste
½ teaspoon *garam masala* powder
2 teaspoons chopped fresh coriander

Method

1. Heat half the oil in a non-stick pan; add the onion, half the tomato and ginger-garlic paste and sauté till fragrant. Cool and grind to a fine paste. Set aside.
2. Heat the remaining oil in another non-stick pan. Add the remaining tomato and salt and sauté on medium heat for four to five minutes or till tomato is tender and the oil separates from the mixture.
3. Add the coriander powder, chilli powder and turmeric powder and sauté for a minute. Add the green peas, mushrooms and sauté on medium heat for five more minutes.
4. Add the ground paste and boiled potatoes and bring to a boil. Cook on low heat for five minutes, stirring continuously.
5. Add the cashew nut paste and *garam masala* powder and let it simmer for another three minutes, stirring continuously.
6. Garnish with the chopped coriander and serve hot.

• **Preparation time:** 20-25 minutes • **Cooking time:** 30-35 minutes • **Serves:** 4

Ajwaini Arbi

Ingredients

¼ teaspoon carom seeds (*ajwain*)
½ kg taro/colocasia (*arbi*)
1 tablespoon oil + 6 tablespoons for deep-frying
2 tablespoons ginger, chopped
2-3 green chillies
Rock salt to taste
¼ teaspoon red chilli powder
A pinch dried mango powder (*amchur*)
¼ teaspoon coriander powder

Method

1. Boil the *arbi* till soft. Flatten the *arbi* on a wooden board.
2. Heat six tablespoons of oil in a non-stick pan and deep-fry the *arbi* till they turn brown on both sides. Drain the *arbi* on absorbent paper.
3. Grind together the ginger and green chillies to make a paste.
4. Heat one tablespoon of oil in a non-stick pan. Add *ajwain* and when it starts crackling, add ginger-chilli paste. Stir-fry for few minutes.
5. Add the fried *arbi* and stir-fry on low heat. Add the rock salt, chilli powder, dried mango powder and coriander powder and mix. Serve hot.

• **Preparation time:** 15 minutes • **Cooking time:** 15 minutes • **Serves:** 4

Main Dishes
Non-Vegetarian

Palm Court

होटल कनिष्क
Hotel Kanishka

Chicken Keema

Ingredients

500 grams minced chicken (*keema*)
2 tablespoons oil
2 medium onions, chopped
2 tablespoons ginger-garlic paste
Salt to taste
1 teaspoon red chilli powder
1 teaspoon powdered dried fenugreek leaves (*kasoori methi*)
¼ teaspoon turmeric powder
¼ cup tomato purée
½ teaspoon *garam masala* powder

Method

1. Heat the oil in a non-stick pan; add the onions and sauté till lightly browned. Add the ginger-garlic paste and sauté on medium heat for a minute.
2. Add the chicken, salt, chilli powder, dried fenugreek leaves and turmeric powder. Mix well and cook, stirring continuously, to prevent the mince from scorching.
3. Add the tomato purée and cook on medium heat till the purée is absorbed.
4. Add one cup water, cover the pan and cook till the chicken is tender. Add *garam masala* powder and mix.
5. Serve hot, preferably with *parantha*.

• **Preparation time:** 10-15 minutes • **Cooking time:** 25-30 minutes • **Serves:** 4

Chicken Badam Pasanda

Ingredients

600 grams chicken *pasande*
¼ cup oil

Marinade

1 egg
Salt to taste
½ teaspoon red chilli powder
2 teaspoons lemon juice
5 teaspoons ginger-garlic paste

For curry

¼ cup almonds, blanched
½ cup yogurt
¼ cup oil
1 tablespoon butter
1 tablespoon ginger-garlic paste
Salt to taste
1½ teaspoons red chilli powder
½ teaspoon white pepper powder
2 tablespoons browned onion paste
¼ cup tomato purée
¼ cup fresh cream

For garnishing

1 teaspoon fresh cream
3-4 almonds, slivered
A pinch *garam masala* powder

Method

1. For the marinade, whip the egg with salt, chilli powder, lemon juice and ginger-garlic paste. Set aside.
2. Flatten out each *pasanda* with a wooden mallet and coat with the prepared marinade. Marinate for fifteen minutes in a refrigerator. Heat the oil in a non-stick pan and shallow-fry the chicken *pasande* until golden on both sides. Drain on absorbent paper.
3. For the curry, grind the almonds to a fine paste and blend with yogurt. Heat the oil with the butter in a non-stick pan; add the ginger-garlic paste and sauté for a few seconds.
4. Add the yogurt-almond mixture and sauté, stirring continuously. Add the salt, chilli powder and white pepper powder and sauté for one to two minutes. Remove the pan from heat. Stir in the browned onion paste, tomato purée and cream and mix well. Return the pan to heat and sauté on medium heat for eight to ten minutes.
5. Add the chicken *pasande* and cook on low heat till the *pasande* are tender and the curry is reduced to half. Remove the chicken pieces from the curry and place on a serving platter. Pour the curry on top of the pieces.
6. Garnish with a swirl of cream, sprinkle the slivered almonds and the *garam masala* powder and serve hot.

• **Preparation time:** 20-25 minutes • **Cooking time:** 40-45 minutes • **Serves:** 4

Butter Chicken

Ingredients

1 kg readymade *tandoori* chicken, cut into 2-inch pieces

½ cup butter

3-4 medium tomatoes, chopped

1 bay leaf

2 tablespoons cashew nut powder

4 teaspoons tomato sauce

¼ teaspoon red chilli powder

2 inches ginger, chopped

1 teaspoon sugar

Salt to taste

½ cup fresh cream

2 teaspoons chopped fresh coriander

2 green chillies, slit

Method

1. Boil the tomatoes in one cup of water and bay leaf for five to seven minutes.
2. Remove and discard the bay leaf. Cool and purée the tomatoes.
3. Melt the butter in a non-stick pan; add the cashew nut powder and cook till golden brown. Reduce the heat and add the fresh tomato purée, tomato sauce, chilli powder, ginger, sugar and salt.
4. Mix well and bring it to a boil. Add the chicken and mix gently.
5. When the gravy comes to a boil again, remove the pan from heat and add the cream.
6. Transfer into a serving bowl.
7. Serve hot, garnished with the chopped coriander and green chillies.

• **Preparation time:** 30-35 minutes • **Cooking time:** 45-50 minutes • **Serves:** 4

Chicken Chettinaad

Ingredients

500 grams boneless chicken, cut into 1½-inch pieces

10 dried red chillies

1 black cardamom

2 cloves

½ fresh coconut, grated

4 teaspoons coconut oil

1 teaspoon garlic paste

5 sprigs curry leaves

1 green cardamom, crushed

Salt to taste

Method

1. Dry-roast the red chillies, black cardamom and cloves. Cool and grind with the coconut and a little water to a fine paste.
2. Heat the coconut oil in a non-stick pan; add the garlic paste, curry leaves, crushed green cardamom and the ground paste.
3. Add the chicken and sauté on medium heat for three to four minutes. Add one cup of water and salt and mix. Cover the pan and cook for twenty minutes on low heat.
4. Transfer into a serving dish and serve hot with boiled rice.

Chef's Tip

The chilli factor in *chicken chettinaad* can be lowered by reducing the quantity of dried red chillies.

• **Preparation time:** 30-35 minutes • **Cooking time:** 1 hour • **Serves:** 4

Chicken Saagwala

Ingredients

800 grams chicken on the bone, cut into 2-inch pieces

1 medium bunch (350 grams) fresh spinach leaves, trimmed

2 tablespoons oil

2 teaspoons cumin seeds

1 bay leaf

4 teaspoons ginger-garlic paste

½ cup onion paste

½ cup tomato purée

Salt to taste

½ teaspoon *garam masala* powder

1 teaspoon red chilli powder

1 teaspoon coriander powder

2 teaspoons fresh cream

Method

1. Blanch the spinach leaves in sufficient hot water for two minutes. Drain, refresh under running water, drain well again and purée.
2. Heat the oil in a non-stick pan; add the cumin seeds and when they change colour, add the bay leaf and ginger-garlic paste and sauté for a minute.
3. Add the onion paste and sauté for two minutes. Add the chicken and sauté till they are lightly browned.
4. Reduce the heat and cook, stirring occasionally, till the chicken is tender.
5. Add the tomato purée and cook till the oil separates. Add the salt, *garam masala* powder, chilli powder and coriander powder. Mix well.
6. Add the spinach and cook for two to three minutes.
7. Serve hot, garnished with the cream.

• **Preparation time:** 15-20 minutes • **Cooking time:** 25-30 minutes • **Serves:** 4

Murgh Kandhari

Ingredients

600 grams boneless chicken, cut into 1-inch pieces

4 teaspoons ginger-garlic paste

Salt to taste

1 teaspoon red chilli powder

½ cup oil

2 tablespoons cashew nut paste

4 teaspoons yogurt

4 teaspoons browned onion paste

1 tablespoon tomato purée

½ cup fresh pomegranate kernels

4 teaspoons fresh cream

½ teaspoon *garam masala* powder

Method

1. Marinate the chicken with two teaspoons ginger-garlic paste, salt and half teaspoon chilli powder for ten to fifteen minutes.
2. Heat one-fourth cup oil in a non-stick pan; add the marinated chicken and sauté for a few minutes without letting the colour change. Drain and set aside.
3. Add the remaining oil to the pan; add the remaining ginger-garlic paste and sauté for two to three minutes. Add the cashew nut paste mixed with yogurt and one cup water and mix well. Add salt and remaining chilli powder.
4. Simmer for eight to ten minutes. Add the browned onion paste, tomato purée and chicken and cook on low heat till the chicken is tender and the gravy thickens.
5. Extract juice from the pomegranate kernels and strain through a piece of muslin into the gravy and mix well.
6. Remove the pan from heat and stir in the cream.
7. Transfer into a serving dish, sprinkle the *garam masala* powder and serve hot.

• **Preparation time:** 20-25 minutes • **Cooking time:** 25-30 minutes • **Serves:** 4

Keema Curry

Ingredients

500 grams minced lamb
½ cup oil
2 medium onion, chopped
2 teaspoons ginger paste
2 teaspoons garlic paste
2 green chillies, chopped
½ teaspoon turmeric powder
2 teaspoon cumin powder
Salt to taste
½ cup tomato purée
¼ cup chopped fresh coriander

Method

1. Heat the oil in a non-stick pan; add the onion and sauté till lightly browned.
2. Add the mince and sauté on medium heat till it turns brown.
3. Add the ginger paste, garlic paste and green chillies and sauté for five minutes. Add the turmeric powder and cumin powder and sauté for two minutes more, adding a little water if required.
4. Add the tomato purée and bring the mixture to a boil. Lower the heat and simmer uncovered for fifteen minutes or till the mince is cooked.
5. Serve hot garnished with chopped coriander.

• **Preparation time:** 15 minutes • **Cooking time:** 30 minutes • **Serves:** 4

Laziz Pasliyan

Ingredients

16 lamb ribs (*pasliyan*)

For gravy

1 cup ghee
8-9 medium onions, chopped
1 teaspoon green cardamom powder
7-8 cloves
2 one-inch sticks cinnamon
5 bay leaves
2 tablespoons ginger-garlic paste
4-5 medium tomatoes, finely chopped
2 teaspoons *garam masala* powder
1 tablespoon coriander powder
2 teaspoons red chilli powder
½ teaspoon turmeric powder
Salt to taste
4 teaspoons cashew nut paste
½ cup yogurt, whisked

For garnish

4 teaspoons chopped fresh mint leaves
4 inches ginger, cut into thin strips

Method

1. Heat the ghee in deep non-stick pan; add the onions and sauté over medium heat.
2. Add the cardamom powder, cloves, cinnamon, bay leaves, ginger-garlic paste, tomatoes, *garam masala* powder, coriander powder, chilli powder, turmeric powder, salt and cashew nut paste and mix well. Sauté till the oil separates.
3. Add the yogurt and the ribs, cover and cook on medium heat, stirring occasionally, for forty to forty-five minutes, or till the ribs are tender and the gravy thick.
4. Serve hot, garnished with mint leaves and ginger strips.

• **Preparation time:** 30-35 minutes • **Cooking time:** 1 hour • **Serves:** 4

Nargisi Kofta

Ingredients

500 grams minced lamb (*keema*)
8 eggs, boiled and shelled
5 teaspoons gram flour (*besan*)
4 teaspoons garlic-ginger paste
1 teaspoon red chilli powder
1 teaspoon cumin powder
1 teaspoon coriander powder
Salt to taste
Oil for deep-frying
2 tablespoons chopped fresh coriander

For gravy

1 tablespoon oil
1 tablespoon butter
¼ cup onion paste
2 tablespoons ginger-garlic paste
3-4 medium tomatoes, chopped
1 teaspoon turmeric powder
1 teaspoon red chilli powder
1 teaspoon *garam masala* powder
Salt to taste
1 cup yogurt

Method

1. Combine the gram flour, garlic-ginger paste, chilli powder, cumin powder, coriander powder and salt with the minced lamb and mix well.
2. Evenly coat each boiled egg well with this mixture.
3. Heat sufficient oil in a *kadai* and deep-fry the mince-coated eggs (*nargisi kofta*) till golden. Drain on absorbent paper and set aside.
4. For the gravy, heat the oil and butter in a non-stick pan; add the onion paste and ginger-garlic paste and sauté till fragrant.
5. Add the tomatoes, turmeric powder, chilli powder, *garam masala* powder and salt and sauté till the oil separates. Add the *kofte* and yogurt and mix gently. Let the mixture simmer on low heat for ten minutes.
6. Cut each *kofta* into half horizontally and place in a serving dish. Pour the gravy over them, garnish with the chopped coriander and serve hot.

• **Preparation time:** 25-30 minutes • **Cooking time:** 1 hour • **Serves:** 4

Shahi Korma

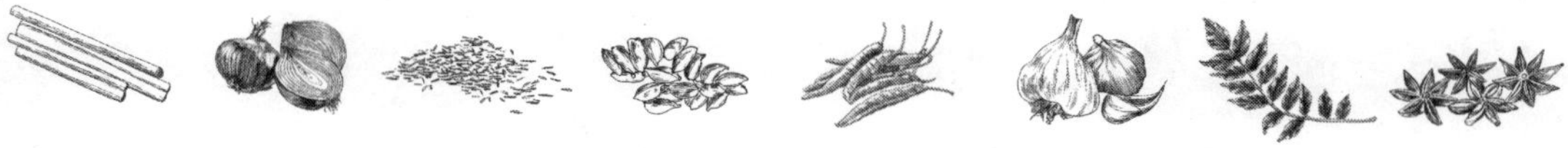

Ingredients

500 grams boneless lamb leg pieces, cut into 2-inch pieces
2 tablespoons almond paste
2 tablespoons cashew nut paste
1 teaspoon poppy seed (*khus khus*) paste
1 teaspoon green cardamom powder
½ cup ghee
3 medium onions, grated
4-5 garlic cloves, grated
1 inch ginger, grated
1 teaspoon *garam masala* powder
1 teaspoon red chilli powder
Salt to taste
1 cup milk
1 tablespoon chopped fresh coriander
4-5 almonds, chopped

Method

1. Lightly roast the almond paste, cashew nut paste, poppy seed paste and cardamom powder in a non-stick pan till fragrant. Set aside.
2. Heat the ghee in another non-stick pan and add the onions, garlic and ginger and sauté till onions turn golden.
3. Add the lamb pieces and sauté on medium heat for five minutes.
4. Add the *garam masala* powder and chilli powder and mix. Sauté, stirring continuously, till the oil separates. Add the salt and two cups water, increase heat, cover the pan and cook till meat is tender.
5. Take the pan off the heat, uncover and add milk and the roasted pastes.
6. Cook on low heat, stirring continuously, ensuring that the gravy does not come to a boil.
7. Transfer the *korma* into a serving dish.
8. Garnish with the chopped coriander and almonds and serve hot.

• **Preparation time:** 30-35 minutes • **Cooking time:** 1 hour • **Serves:** 4

Rogan Josh

Ingredients

750 grams lamb leg on the bone, cut into 1½-inch pieces

½ cup ghee

1 teaspoon asafoetida (*hing*)

2 one-inch sticks cinnamon

6-8 cloves

6-8 black peppercorns

4 black cardamoms

2 teaspoons Kashmiri red chilli powder

2 teaspoons fennel (*saunf*) powder

1 tablespoon dried ginger powder (*saunth*)

1 tablespoon coriander powder

Salt to taste

1 cup yogurt, whisked

Method

1. Heat the ghee in a deep non-stick pan. Add the asafoetida, cinnamon, cloves, peppercorns and black cardamoms and sauté till fragrant.
2. Add the lamb pieces and sauté on medium heat, stirring continuously, for about fifteen minutes or till the lamb pieces turn reddish brown.
3. Each time the lamb pieces begin to stick to the bottom of the pan sprinkle a little water, stir continuously and continue cooking on low heat till the ghee begins to separate.
4. Add the chilli powder, fennel powder, dried ginger powder, coriander powder and salt and mix well.
5. Add the yogurt and two cups of water and mix. Cover and cook on medium heat, till the lamb is tender, stirring occasionally for forty to forty-five minutes.
6. Serve hot with boiled rice.

• **Preparation time:** 15-20 minutes • **Cooking time:** 1¼ hour • **Serves:** 4

Saag Gosht

Ingredients

500 grams lamb leg on the bone, cut into 1-inch pieces

4 bunches (350 grams each approx.) fresh spinach leaves, trimmed

2 tablespoons oil

3-4 medium onions, grated

5 garlic cloves, grated

½ inch ginger, grated

1½ teaspoons red chilli powder

¼ teaspoon green cardamom powder

1 teaspoon *garam masala* powder

3 medium tomatoes, blanched and chopped

Salt to taste

½ cup fresh cream

2 teaspoons lemon juice

Method

1. Blanch the spinach in five cups of water on high heat for five minutes. Drain, refresh under running water, drain and purée. Set aside.
2. Heat the oil in a non-stick pan; add the onions and sauté till golden. Add the garlic and ginger and continue to sauté.
3. Reduce heat, add the chilli powder, cardamom powder and *garam masala* powder and mix well.
4. Add the tomatoes and sauté till the oil separates. Add the lamb and cook, sprinkling little water at intervals to prevent scorching of the lamb or its sticking to the base of the pan.
5. Add two cups water and salt, cover pan and cook on high heat till the lamb pieces are tender. Add the spinach purée and cook on medium heat till the oil separates.
6. Remove the pan from heat, stir in the cream, and return the pan to low heat and cook for five minutes.
7. Transfer into a serving bowl, add the lemon juice and garnish with strips of ginger. Serve hot.

• **Preparation time:** 30-35 minutes • **Cooking time:** 1 hour • **Serves:** 4

Baoli Handi

Ingredients

500 grams boneless lamb, cut into ¾-inch cubes

¼ cup oil

2 one-inch sticks cinnamon

5 cloves

A pinch of nutmeg powder

4 green cardamoms

3 tablespoons ginger-garlic paste

2-3 medium onions, chopped

Salt to taste

1 teaspoon red chilli powder

¾ teaspoon *garam masala* powder

1½ teaspoons coriander powder

1 teaspoon turmeric powder

1 cup fresh tomato purée

2 tablespoons grated cottage cheese (*paneer*)

¼ cup yogurt

¼ cup browned onion paste

½ cup shelled green peas

1 medium carrot, sliced

8-10 medium fresh button mushrooms, chopped

¼ cup chopped cashew nuts

Method

1. Heat the oil in a large non-stick pan; add the cinnamon, cloves, nutmeg powder and green cardamoms and sauté till fragrant. Add the ginger-garlic paste and sauté for three to five minutes.

2. Add the lamb cubes and onions and sauté on medium heat till all the moisture dries up. Add the salt, chilli powder, *garam masala* powder, coriander powder and turmeric powder and mix well. Add the tomato purée and sauté till the oil separates from the gravy.

3. Add the cottage cheese, yogurt and browned onion paste. Add two cups water, cover and cook till the mutton is tender. Add the green peas, carrot, mushrooms and cashew nuts. Stir well and cook for five minutes.

4. Transfer into a serving dish and serve hot with boiled rice or bread.

• **Preparation time:** 20-25 minutes • **Cooking time:** 1 hour • **Serves:** 4

Gosht Aur Mirchi Ka Saalan

Ingredients

½ kg boneless mutton, cut into 1½-inch pieces

10 large green chillies

Salt to taste

7 tablespoons oil

3 teaspoons cumin seeds

1 teaspoon onion seeds (*kalonji*)

1 cup chopped fresh coriander

For paste

½ cup tamarind pulp

1 teaspoon turmeric powder

2 teaspoons chilli powder

1 teaspoon aniseeds, roasted

1 teaspoon *garam masala* powder

1 teaspoon poppy seeds

1 tablespoon ginger-garlic paste

1 teaspoon sesame seeds, roasted

2 onions, chopped

2 tomatoes, chopped

Method

1. For the paste, grind together all the ingredients. Marinate the mutton in the paste alongwith salt for thirty minutes
2. Heat five tablespoons of oil in a pressure cooker. Add the cumin seeds and onion seeds. When they start crackling, add the mutton alongwith the *masala*. Fry till the oil separates.
3. Add two cups of hot water and pressure-cook till the meat is done. This will take about fifteeen minutes.
4. Heat the remaining oil in a non-stick pan and fry the green chillies till they soften. Add to the meat and let the mixture simmer for three to four minutes.
5. Garnish with chopped coriander.

• **Preparation time:** 30 minutes • **Cooking time:** 60 minutes • **Serves:** 4

Machher Jhol

Ingredients

2 large pomfrets, cut into 2-inch thick pieces

1 teaspoon turmeric powder

Salt to taste

4 tablespoons filtered mustard oil

⅓ teaspoon fenugreek seeds (*methi dana*)

½ teaspoon cumin seeds

4 bay leaves

2 medium onions, chopped

4 teaspoons ginger-garlic paste

2 medium tomatoes, chopped

2 green chillies, chopped

¾ teaspoon red chilli powder

1⅓ teaspoons coriander powder

1 teaspoon chopped fresh coriander

Method

1. Apply half a teaspoon turmeric powder and salt on the fish and set aside.
2. Heat the mustard oil in a non-stick pan and shallow-fry the fish on both sides till three-fourth done. Drain and set aside.
3. Add the fenugreek seeds and cumin seeds to the oil remaining in the pan, sauté till they change colour. Add the bay leaves and onions and sauté on medium heat till golden.
4. Add the ginger-garlic paste and sauté for a minute. Add the tomatoes and sauté till the oil separates.
5. Add the green chillies, salt, chilli powder and coriander powder and mix well. Sauté on low heat for two to three minutes. Increase heat, add one cup of water and bring to a boil.
6. Add the fish and let it simmer, covered, on low heat for ten to fifteen minutes, till fish is cooked and the gravy thickens.
7. Transfer into a serving dish and serve hot, garnished with the chopped coriander.

• **Preparation time:** 20-25 minutes • **Cooking time:** 40-45 minutes • **Serves:** 4

Prawn Malai Curry

Ingredients

16 large prawns, shelled and deveined
1 coconut, freshly grated
3 tablespoons oil
2 teaspoons ginger-garlic paste
1 teaspoon red chilli powder
1 teaspoon coriander powder
1 teaspoon turmeric powder
2 sprigs curry leaves
Salt to taste
¼ cup yogurt, whisked
¼ cup tomato purée
⅓ teaspoon *garam masala* powder
1 teaspoon chopped fresh coriander

Method

1. Grind the coconut with one cup of warm water; transfer into a piece of muslin and squeeze the milk into a bowl and set aside.
2. Heat the oil in a non-stick pan, add the ginger-garlic paste, chilli powder, coriander powder, turmeric powder, curry leaves and salt and sauté for two to three minutes.
3. Stir in the yogurt and tomato purée; mix well and cook for about five to seven minutes.
4. Add the prawns and cook for two to three minutes.
5. Add one cup of water and cook till the prawns are tender and the gravy thickens.
6. Add the *garam masala* powder and coconut milk. Let it simmer for five minutes.
7. Transfer into a serving dish and garnish with the chopped coriander. Serve hot.

• **Preparation time:** 10-15 minutes • **Cooking time:** 30-35 minutes • **Serves:** 4

Shrimp Jhalfraezi

Ingredients

1½ cups shrimps, shelled and deveined
1 teaspoon coriander powder
2 garlic cloves, crushed
Salt to taste
1 tablespoon oil
½ teaspoon cumin seeds
2 green chillies, slit
Black pepper powder, as required
½ teaspoon cumin powder
1 medium green capsicum, sliced
1 medium red capsicum, sliced
1 medium yellow capsicum, sliced
2 medium tomatoes, sliced
2 teaspoons chopped fresh coriander

Method

1. Pat the shrimps dry and marinate them with the coriander powder, garlic and salt for fifteen minutes.
2. Heat the oil in a non-stick pan; add the cumin seeds and sauté till they change colour. Add the green chillies and the marinated shrimps and sauté for five minutes, stirring continuously. Add the pepper powder and cumin powder.
3. Add the green, red and yellow capsicums and tomatoes and mix. Cook on low heat for ten minutes.
4. Transfer into a serving dish, garnish with the chopped coriander and serve with boiled rice.

• **Preparation time:** 10-15 minutes • **Cooking time:** 25-30 minutes • **Serves:** 4

Crab Curry

Ingredients

4 medium crabs, cleaned
¼ cup oil
25 Kashmiri red chillies
1 tablespoon coriander seeds
1 coconut, freshly grated
2 teaspoons cumin seeds
8-10 black peppercorns
1 teaspoon fenugreek seeds (*methi dana*)
½ teaspoon turmeric powder
4-5 garlic cloves, chopped
¼ cup tamarind pieces
1 tablespoon coconut oil
1 medium onion, chopped
Salt to taste

Method

1. Heat the oil in non-stick pan and sauté red chillies, coriander seeds, coconut, cumin seeds, peppercorns and fenugreek seeds till fragrant. Cool and grind them with the turmeric powder and garlic to a fine paste.
2. Soak the tamarind in one cup of water till they become soft. Mash well and strain the juice. Set aside. Heat the coconut oil in a deep non-stick pan; add the onion and sauté till lightly browned.
3. Add the crabs and sauté till their colour changes. Add the ground paste and salt and mix well. Sauté for two minutes stirring continuously.
4. Add the tamarind juice and cook on low heat for five minutes.
5. Serve hot with boiled rice.

• **Preparation time:** 25-30 minutes • **Cooking time:** 45-50 minutes • **Serves:** 4

Prawn Balchao

Ingredients

500 grams medium prawns, shelled and deveined
A pinch of turmeric powder
Salt to taste
2 tablespoons oil
1 sprig curry leaves
4 medium onions, finely chopped
4 medium tomatoes, finely chopped
2 green chillies, chopped
2 tablespoons sugar
1 tablespoon vinegar

For paste

2 teaspoons ginger-garlic paste
2 dried red chillies
2 teaspoons vinegar
½ teaspoon turmeric powder
2 teaspoons cumin seeds
2 teaspoons mustard seeds
20 black peppercorns

Method

1. Rub the prawns with a pinch of turmeric powder and little salt and set aside for five minutes. Wash them well and pat them dry.
2. For the paste, grind together the ginger-garlic paste, red chillies, vinegar, turmeric powder, cumin seeds, mustard seeds and peppercorns. Rub the prawns with this paste and set aside to marinate for fifteen minutes.
3. Heat the oil in a large non-stick frying pan and add the curry leaves.
4. Add the onions and sauté on medium heat till they are lightly browned.
5. Add the tomatoes and sauté till the oil separates.
6. Add the prawns with the marinade and cook for two minutes, stirring occasionally.
7. Add the green chillies, sugar, salt and vinegar. Mix well, cover the pan and cook on low heat for ten minutes. Serve hot.

• **Preparation time:** 30-35 minutes • **Cooking time:** 45-50 minutes • **Serves:** 4

Fish Moilee

Ingredients

500 grams fish fillets
1 teaspoon turmeric powder
Salt to taste
2 teaspoons coconut oil + for shallow-frying
½ teaspoon mustard seeds
1 medium onion, sliced
2-3 garlic cloves, chopped
1 inch ginger, chopped
2-3 green chillies
2 sprigs curry leaves
1 medium tomato, sliced
1 teaspoon black pepper powder
1 teaspoon lemon juice/vinegar
1 teaspoon red chilli powder
2 cups coconut milk

Method

1. Pat the fish dry, sprinkle the turmeric powder and salt and set aside for fifteen minutes.
2. Heat sufficient coconut oil in a non-stick frying pan and shallow-fry fish fillets till golden. Drain on absorbent paper.
3. Heat two teaspoons coconut oil in another non-stick pan; add the mustard seeds. When they start spluttering, add the onion, garlic and ginger and sauté till the onion turns light brown.
4. Add the green chillies, curry leaves and sauté for a minute. Add the tomato and sauté for a minute longer taking care that the tomato does not get mashed.
5. Add the pepper powder, one-fourth cup water, lemon juice/vinegar, chilli powder and salt and cook on low heat for two minutes.
6. Add the coconut milk and simmer until the gravy thickens slightly.
7. Carefully place fried fillets into the gravy and cook for two to three minutes.
8. Serve with boiled rice.

• **Preparation time:** 30-35 minutes • **Cooking time:** 30-35 minutes • **Serves:** 4

Fish Kofte

Ingredients

500 grams rohu fish
2 eggs
3 medium onions, grated
1 teaspoon ginger-garlic paste
1 teaspoon red chilli powder
2 teaspoons turmeric powder
Salt to taste
Filtered mustard oil for deep-frying
2 teaspoons chopped fresh coriander

For gravy

3 medium onions, chopped
2 large tomatoes, chopped
2-3 green chillies, chopped
1 tablespoon vinegar
2 tablespoons chopped fresh coriander
2 tablespoons oil

Method

1. For the *kofte*, boil the fish in five cups of water till soft. Drain the fish and reserve the cooking liquid. Remove the bones and mash the flesh and put it in a bowl.
2. Add the eggs, onions, ginger-garlic paste, chilli powder, turmeric powder and salt to the fish.
3. Mix well, divide into equal portions and shape them into oblong-shaped *kofte*.
4. Heat sufficient mustard oil in a *kadai* and deep-fry the *kofte* till golden. Drain on absorbent paper and set aside.
5. For the gravy, grind together the onions, tomatoes, green chillies, vinegar and chopped coriander and set aside.
6. Heat the oil in a non-stick pan; add the ground onion-tomato paste and sauté till the oil separates.
7. Add the *kofte* and the reserved cooking liquid and cook on low heat for five minutes.
8. Garnish with the chopped coriander and serve hot.

• **Preparation time:** 30-35 minutes • **Cooking time:** 30-35 minutes • **Serves:** 4

Rice & Bread

Palm Court

होटल कनिष्क
Hotel Kanishka

Vegetable Pulao

Ingredients

1½ cups Basmati rice, soaked
1 medium carrot, cut into tiny cubes
10-12 French beans, cut into 1-inch pieces
1 medium green capsicum, chopped
½ cup cauliflower florets
2 medium tomatoes, chopped
½ cup shelled green peas
2 tablespoons ghee
4 black cardamoms
1 teaspoon caraway seeds (*shahi jeera*)
3 bay leaves
2 one-inch sticks cinnamon
2 cloves
2 blades mace (*javitri*)
Salt to taste
1 cup fried cashew nuts
5 teaspoons raisins (*kishmish*), chopped
A few saffron threads

Method

1. Boil the rice in five cups of water till cooked. Drain and divide into two equal portions and set aside.
2. Heat half the ghee in a non-stick pan; add the black cardamoms, caraway seeds, bay leaves, cinnamon, cloves and mace and sauté on medium heat till fragrant.
3. Add the carrot, French beans, capsicum, cauliflower, tomatoes, green peas and salt, mix well and sauté on a medium heat for two minutes.
4. Remove from heat, let it cool and divide this mixture into two equal portions.
5. In a large non-stick pan, spread one portion of rice and cover with a layer of the sautéed vegetables.
6. Spread the second portion of rice on top of the vegetables and cover with the remaining vegetables. Drizzle the remaining ghee, sprinkle fried cashew nuts, raisins and saffron evenly on top. Cover and cook on low heat for fifteen minutes.
7. Serve hot with *raita*.

• **Preparation time:** 45-50 minutes • **Cooking time:** 1 hour • **Serves:** 4

Vegetable Biryani

Ingredients

1½ cups Basmati rice, soaked
1 medium potato, chopped
1 medium carrot, chopped
1 cup shelled green peas
Salt to taste
2 teaspoons butter
2 teaspoons oil
2 medium onions, chopped
6-8 garlic cloves, chopped
2 inches ginger, chopped
½ teaspoon cumin powder
1 teaspoon turmeric powder
½ teaspoon curry powder
1 teaspoon red chilli powder
¼ cup yogurt, whisked
3-4 green chillies, chopped
1 small tomato, chopped
½ cup chopped fresh coriander

Method

1. Drain and boil the rice in five cups of water with salt till almost cooked. Drain and set aside.
2. Melt the butter with oil in a non-stick pan; add the onions and sauté till translucent.
3. Add the garlic and ginger and sauté for one minute. Add the cumin powder, turmeric powder, curry powder and chilli powder; stir and sauté for a minute.
4. Add the potato, carrot, two cups of water and salt. Let the mixture simmer till the water evaporates and the vegetables are tender.
5. Stir in the green peas and remove pan from heat. Add the yogurt and rice and mix well.
6. Serve hot, garnished with the green chillies, tomato and chopped coriander.

• **Preparation time:** 30-35 minutes • **Cooking time:** 30-35 minutes • **Serves:** 4

Lemon Rice

Ingredients

3 cups cooked rice
2 teaspoons lemon juice
A pinch of turmeric powder
Salt to taste
3 teaspoons sesame (*til*) oil
1 teaspoon mustard seeds
1 teaspoon skinless split black gram (*dhuli urad dal*)
1 teaspoon split Bengal gram (*chana dal*)
3-5 dried red chillies
¼ teaspoon asafoetida
½ cup roasted peanuts
4-5 curry leaves

Method

1. Place the rice in a bowl; add the turmeric powder, salt and one teaspoon of sesame oil and mix well.
2. Heat the remaining sesame oil in a non-stick pan and add mustard seeds. When the seeds splutter, add the split black gram, split Bengal gram, red chillies, asafoetida, roasted peanuts and curry leaves.
3. Add the rice. Mix well and toss for a minute. Add the lemon juice and toss again. Serve hot.

• **Preparation time:** 15-20 minutes • **Cooking time:** 10-15 minutes • **Serves:** 4

Curd Rice

Ingredients

3 cups cooked rice
3 cups yogurt (*curd/dahi*)
4 teaspoons oil
1 teaspoon mustard seeds
3-4 curry leaves
2-3 dried red chillies
Salt to taste
Lemon pickle/mango pickle, for serving

Method

1. Heat the oil in a non-stick pan; add the mustard seeds, curry leaves and dried red chillies and sauté till the seeds splutter. Lower the heat; add the yogurt and salt.
2. Add the rice and stir well. Remove the pan from heat.
3. Transfer the rice into a serving plate. Serve cold with lemon pickle/mango pickle.

• **Preparation time:** 15-20 minutes • **Cooking time:** 15-20 minutes • **Serves:** 4

Tamarind Rice

Ingredients

3 cups cooked rice
1 cup tamarind
¼ cup split Bengal gram (*chana dal*)
1 teaspoon skinless split black gram (*dhuli urad dal*)
Salt to taste
2 tablespoons coconut oil
¼ teaspoon turmeric powder
¼ cup peanuts
2 green chillies, chopped
5 dried red chillies
4-5 curry leaves
2 teaspoons mustard seeds
1 teaspoon cumin seeds
A pinch asafoetida (*hing*)

Method

1. Soak the tamarind in one cup of warm water and extract the juice. Discard the seeds and pulp.
2. Soak the split Bengal gram and split black gram in water for half an hour. Drain and set aside. Add the salt and two teaspoons of coconut oil to the rice and mix well.
3. Pour the tamarind juice in a non-stick pan; add the salt and turmeric powder. Cook till the mixture thickens. Add this to the rice and mix.
4. Heat the remaining oil in a non-stick pan; add the split Bengal gram, split black gram, peanuts, green chillies, red chillies, curry leaves, mustard seeds, cumin seeds and asafoetida. Sauté over medium heat till the ingredients turn brown.
5. Add the rice and mix well. Toss for three to four minutes. Serve hot.

• **Preparation time:** 15-20 minutes • **Cooking time:** 20-25 minutes • **Serves:** 4

Coconut Rice

Ingredients

3 cups cooked rice
2 cups freshly grated coconut
3 teaspoons sesame (*til*) oil
1 teaspoon mustard seeds
2 teaspoons skinless split black gram (*dhuli urad dal*)
2 teaspoons split Bengal gram (*chana dal*)
3-5 dried red chillies
1 cup chopped cashew nuts
¼ teaspoon asafoetida (*hing*)
Salt to taste
4 sprigs curry leaves

Method

1. Heat the oil in a non-stick pan; add the mustard seeds and let them splutter. Add the split black gram, split Bengal gram, red chillies, cashew nuts and asafoetida and sauté till both the *dal* turn a light brown.
2. Add the coconut and sauté till it turns light brown in colour. Add the cooked rice and salt and mix well.
3. Transfer the coconut rice into a serving plate and garnish with the curry leaves.
4. Serve hot.

• **Preparation time:** 15-20 minutes • **Cooking time:** 10-15 minutes • **Serves:** 4

Chicken Biryani

Ingredients

600 grams chicken, cut into 1½-inch pieces on the bone

1½ cups Basmati rice, soaked for ½ hour and drained

3 tablespoons oil

2 teaspoons ginger-garlic paste

Salt to taste

3 green cardamoms

3 black cardamoms

3 cloves

2 one-inch sticks cinnamon

4-5 black peppercorns

2 bay leaves

2 medium onions, chopped

2 green chillies, chopped

½ cup yogurt

3 cups chicken stock

½ cup fried sliced onions, for garnish

Method

1. Heat two teaspoons oil in a non-stick pan; add the ginger-garlic paste and chicken. Sauté for five minutes. Add half cup of water and salt. Cover and cook on low heat till the water dries up.
2. Heat the remaining oil in a deep non-stick pan; add both the cardamoms, cloves, cinnamon, peppercorns and bay leaves and sauté till fragrant.
3. Add the onions and sauté till lightly browned. Add the green chillies and chicken and sauté for two minutes.
4. Stir in the yogurt, chicken stock and salt. Bring to a boil, stirring continuously.
5. Reduce heat; add the drained rice and stir till stock reduces to the level of the rice. Cover the pan with a wet cloth. Cook on very low heat (*dum*) until the rice is cooked and the chicken pieces are tender.
6. Remove from heat, transfer into a serving platter, garnish with the fried onions and serve hot.

• **Preparation time:** 1 hour • **Cooking time:** 1 hour • **Serves:** 4

Chilman Biryani

Ingredients

750 grams lamb, cut into 2-inch pieces on the bone

1½ cups Basmati rice, soaked for ½ hour and drained

½ teaspoon mace powder

2 green cardamoms

2 black cardamoms

2-3 cloves

1 bay leaf

4 tablespoons oil

2 medium onions, sliced

5 teaspoons ginger-garlic paste

Salt to taste

2 teaspoons red chilli powder

¼ cup browned onion paste

A few saffron threads

2 teaspoons screw pine essence (*kewda jal*)

½ cup fried sliced onions

For chilman (pastry covering)

½ cup refined flour (*maida*)

½ cup butter

Method

1. Drain and boil the rice in six cups of water with mace powder, cardamoms, cloves and bay leaf till the rice is three-fourth cooked. Drain and set aside.
2. Heat the oil in a deep non-stick pan; add the onions and sauté till golden. Add the ginger-garlic paste and lamb pieces and sauté for eight to ten minutes, stirring continuously.
3. Add the salt, chilli powder and four cups water and cook for twenty to twenty-five minutes on medium heat. Add the browned onion paste and cook till the lamb pieces are tender and gravy thickens. Remove from heat and set aside.
4. To make the pastry covering, mix the flour and butter, add three-fourth cup of water and knead into a soft dough. Arrange the rice and lamb curry in alternate layers in a deep pan. Sprinkle the saffron, *kewda jal* and fried onions.
5. Seal the pan with the prepared pastry and place in an oven preheated at 170°C/325°F/Gas Mark 3 for twenty minutes. Remove the pan from the oven and serve hot.

• **Preparation time:** 35-40 minutes • **Cooking time:** 1 hour 45 minutes • **Serves:** 4

Yakhni Pulao

Ingredients

750 grams lamb, cut into 2-inch pieces
1½ cups Basmati rice, soaked
6 green cardamoms
1 black cardamom
1 teaspoon red chilli powder
6 cloves
1 inch cinnamon
10 black peppercorns
1 teaspoon cumin seeds
2 teaspoons coriander seeds
1 bay leaf
1 star anise
4 teaspoons ginger-garlic paste
Salt to taste
2 tablespoons oil + for deep frying
4 medium onions, chopped
½ cup yogurt, whisked + for serving

Method

1. Place both the cardamoms, chilli powder, cloves, cinnamon, peppercorns, cumin seeds, coriander seeds, bay leaf and star anise in the centre of a six-inch square piece of muslin. Gather up edges of the muslin and tie tightly to form a bundle (*potli*).

2. Heat six cups of water in a deep non-stick pan and place the *potli* in the pan. Add the ginger-garlic paste, lamb and salt and cover. Cook for twenty minutes or till the lamb is almost tender. Remove the *potli*. Strain the lamb and reserve the stock.

3. Heat two tablespoons oil in a non-stick pan; add half the onions and sauté till they turn golden brown. Add the lamb, stock, rice and yogurt and mix well. Cook on medium heat till the mixture comes to a boil. Lower heat, and cover pan with a lid. Cook on low heat till the rice is cooked. Remove from heat and let the rice rest for five minutes.

4. Heat sufficient oil in a *kadai* and deep-fry the remaining onions till golden brown. Drain on absorbent paper.

5. Uncover the pan; stir the rice, taking care not to break the lamb pieces. Garnish with the fried onions and serve hot with yogurt.

• **Preparation time:** 30-35 minutes • **Cooking time:** 40-45 minutes • **Serves:** 4

Anda Parantha

Ingredients

2 cups whole-wheat flour (*atta*)
4 eggs, hard boiled, cooled and peeled
Salt to taste
2 tablespoons chopped fresh coriander
2 green chillies, finely chopped
½ teaspoon black pepper powder
6 eggs, whisked
2 medium onions, chopped
¼ cup oil

Method

1. Sift the flour with salt into a bowl; add enough water and knead into a soft dough. Divide into eight equal portions, cover with a damp cloth and set aside.
2. Grate the boiled eggs into a bowl. Add half the chopped coriander, half the green chillies, salt and pepper powder and mix well. Divide this mixture into eight equal portions.
3. Place the whisked eggs in a bowl and add the onions, salt, remaining chopped coriander and remaining green chillies and mix well.
4. Roll out each dough portion into a *roti*. Place a portion of the filling in the centre, fold in the four ends of the *roti* over each other to make a square envelop.
5. Heat a non-stick *tawa*; place a *parantha* on it. When slightly cooked, turn the *parantha* over and drizzle some of the whisked egg mixture on it. Drizzle a little oil around the edges of the *parantha* and cook till the underside turns golden.
6. Turn the *parantha* over again, drizzle some more of the whisked egg mixture on the *parantha*, drizzle a little oil along the edges and fry till this side also turns golden.
7. Serve hot.

• **Preparation time:** 20-25minutes • **Cooking time:** 30-35 minutes • **Serves:** 4

Aloo Ka Parantha

Ingredients

2 cups whole-wheat flour (*atta*) + for dusting

8 teaspoons butter

Salt to taste

4 tablespoons ghee

For filling

4-5 medium potatoes, boiled, peeled and mashed

1 inch ginger, chopped

2 green chillies, chopped

2 tablespoons chopped fresh coriander

Salt to taste

1 teaspoon red chilli powder

1½ teaspoons powdered dried pomegranate seeds (*anardana*)

For serving

Pickle, as required

Yogurt, as required

Method

1. Mix the butter with the flour; add the salt and knead into a soft dough using water as required. Set aside covered with a damp cloth.
2. For the filling, mix together the potatoes, ginger, green chillies, chopped coriander, salt, chilli powder and dried pomegranate seeds. Divide the filling into eight equal portions. Set aside.
3. Divide the dough into eight equal portions and shape into balls. Shape each ball into a *katori*. Place one portion of the filling in the centre, gather the edges and pinch to seal properly and shape into a ball again.
4. Dust each ball with flour and roll out each ball into an eight-inch round *parantha*.
5. Heat a non-stick *tawa*; place a *parantha* on it. Turn over after one minute, apply a little ghee and cook. Turn it over again and apply a little ghee and cook till both sides are evenly golden and crisp.
6. Serve hot with pickle and yogurt.

• **Preparation time:** 30-35minutes • **Cooking time:** 20-25 minutes • **Serves:** 4

Gobhi Ka Parantha

Ingredients

2 cups whole-wheat flour (*atta*) + for dusting

Salt to taste

1 teaspoon oil

4 tablespoons ghee

For stuffing

1 small cauliflower, grated

Salt to taste

2 teaspoons coriander powder

2 teaspoons cumin powder

1 teaspoon red chilli powder

2 tablespoons chopped fresh coriander

1 green chilli, chopped

1 medium onion, chopped

2 teaspoons ginger-garlic paste

Method

1. For the dough, combine the flour, salt and oil in a bowl, add sufficient water and knead into a soft dough. Divide the dough into eight equal portions, cover with a damp cloth and set aside.
2. For the stuffing, mix the cauliflower with a pinch of salt in a bowl and set aside for ten minutes.
3. Squeeze the cauliflower well to remove any water; add the coriander powder, cumin powder, chilli powder, chopped coriander, green chilli, onion, ginger-garlic paste and salt and mix well. Divide the stuffing into eight equal portions.
4. Roll out each portion of the dough into three-inch diameter *roti*, place a portion of stuffing in the centre, gather the edges and seal to cover the stuffing entirely. Flatten it gently, dust well with extra flour and roll out into a four-inch round *parantha*.
5. Heat a non-stick *tawa*; place each *parantha* over it and cook on medium heat, turning it over and smearing with a little ghee on each side till brown specks appear on both sides. Serve hot with yogurt and pickle.

• **Preparation time:** 15-20 minutes • **Cooking time:** 25-30 minutes • **Serves:** 4

Lachcha Parantha

Ingredients

2 cups refined flour (*maida*) + for dusting

¼ cup milk

1 teaspoon sugar

1 egg, beaten

¼ teaspoon baking powder

1 teaspoon soda bicarbonate

Salt to taste

Ghee for frying

Method

1. Heat the milk in a non-stick pan till warm; add the sugar and stir till it dissolves. Add the egg, baking powder and soda bicarbonate and mix well. Set aside for ten minutes.
2. In a bowl, combine the refined flour and salt. Add the milk mixture, mix well and knead into a dough, adding a little water if required. Divide the dough into eight equal portions and shape into balls.
3. Press each ball into a small disc with your palms, then place it on a greased rolling board and roll it out with a rolling pin evenly on all sides until it is six to seven-inch in diameter. Brush the surface with a little ghee and sprinkle a little flour on it. Pleat it with as many folds as possible.
4. Roll it up into a spiral, flatten lightly and set aside for five minutes. Roll out into six-inch round *parantha*. Heat a non-stick *tawa*; place a *parantha* on it and cook on medium heat on both sides. Drizzle a little ghee and shallow-fry till both sides are golden brown.
5. Crush the *parantha* lightly to open out the layers (*lachche*) and serve hot with any curry.

• **Preparation time:** 20-25 minutes • **Cooking time:** 10-15 minutes • **Serves:** 4

Pudina Parantha

Ingredients

2 cups whole-wheat flour (*atta*)

1 cup fresh mint leaves

Salt to taste

1 tablespoon carom seeds (*ajwain*)

¼ cup ghee

Method

1. Place half a cup of the mint leaves on a heated non-stick pan and dry-roast them on low heat. Set aside to cool. Crush the leaves into a powder. Mix the powder with salt and set aside.
2. Finely chop the remaining mint leaves.
3. Combine the flour, carom seeds, salt, two teaspoons ghee and chopped mint leaves; add sufficient water and knead into a soft dough. Divide the dough into twelve equal portions and shape them into balls.
4. Dust each ball with a little dry flour and roll out into thin *roti*, brush each *roti* with a little ghee and sprinkle a little flour and salt. Pleat it with as many folds as possible, then roll up each into a spiral. Press slightly into a disc and set aside for five minutes. Roll out into a six-inch *parantha*.
5. Heat a non-stick *tawa*, and cook each *parantha*, applying a little ghee on both sides till crisp and golden.
6. Remove from the *tawa*, crush them lightly with your fingers and place on a serving plate. Sprinkle the mint powder on them and serve hot with yogurt and pickle.

• **Preparation time:** 20-25 minutes • **Cooking time:** 20-25 minutes • **Serves:** 4

Sheermal

Ingredients

2 cups refined flour (*maida*)
Salt to taste
2 teaspoons sugar
1 cup warm milk
A few saffron threads
A few drops of screw pine essence (*kewda jal*)
¼ cup ghee
Butter, as required

Method

1. Sift the refined flour with salt into a bowl.
2. Dissolve the sugar in three-fourth cup milk and soak the saffron in the remaining warm milk. Add the sweetened milk and two to three drops of *kewda jal* to the flour and mix well. Add sufficient water and knead into soft dough. Cover with a damp cloth and set aside for ten minutes.
3. Knead the ghee into the dough, cover the dough and set aside for fifteen minutes more.
4. Divide the dough into eight equal portions and shape into balls. Cover and set aside for ten minutes.
5. Preheat oven to 240°C/425°F/Gas Mark 7.
6. Flatten each ball on a lightly floured surface and roll out into six-inch round *roti*. Prick the entire surface lightly with a fork.
7. Grease a baking tray with the butter; arrange the *roti* on it and bake in the preheated oven for five minutes.
8. Remove from the oven; brush the *sheermal* with the saffron-flavoured milk and bake again for three to four minutes.
9. When cooked, remove from oven, brush with butter and serve hot.

• **Preparation time:** 30-35 minutes • **Cooking time:** 30-35 minutes • **Serves:** 4

Bakarkhani

Ingredients

2 cups refined flour (*maida*)
3 teaspoons fresh yeast, crumbled
¾ cup milk
2 teaspoons sugar
10 raisins (*kishmish*)
3 teaspoons cudpahnuts (*chironji*)
½ teaspoon baking powder
Salt to taste
1 teaspoon screw pine essence (*kewda jal*)
½ cup melted ghee + for serving
15 almonds, sliced

Method

1. Dissolve the fresh yeast in quarter cup of warm water. Heat the milk and dissolve the sugar in it. Soak the raisins and *chironji* in half cup of warm water for five minutes, drain and set aside.
2. Sift the refined flour with the baking powder and salt into a bowl. Make a well in the centre, add the sweetened milk, few drops of *kewda jal* and the dissolved yeast and knead into a soft dough. Cover the dough with a damp cloth and set aside for ten minutes.
3. Add one-fourth cup ghee to the dough and knead till it is absorbed. Add the raisins and *chironji*. Knead the dough again and wrap it with a damp cloth and rest for thirty minutes so that the dough rises.
4. Knock back the dough; add the almond slices and knead in the remaining melted ghee. Cover the dough again with the damp cloth and set aside for thirty minutes. Divide the dough into eight equal portions, make balls, cover and set aside for ten to fifteen minutes.
5. Preheat oven to 220°C/425°F/Gas Mark 7.
6. Flatten the balls and roll out into five-inch rounds. Prick the entire surface with a fork. Arrange the discs on a baking tray and bake in the preheated oven for ten minutes.
7. Remove the *bakarkhani* from the oven, brush them with a little ghee and serve hot.

• **Preparation time:** 1 hour plus • **Cooking time:** 10-15 minutes • **Serves:** 4

Missi Roti

Ingredients

1 cup whole-wheat flour (*atta*) + for dusting

1 cup gram flour (*besan*)

2 teaspoons coriander seeds

1 teaspoon dried pomegranate seeds (*anardana*)

1 cup boiled split red lentils (*masoor dal*)

2 medium onions, chopped

2 green chillies, chopped

2 teaspoons chopped fresh coriander

Salt to taste

4 tablespoons oil

Method

1. Roast and grind the coriander seeds and pomegranate seeds separately.
2. Combine the red lentils, ground coriander seeds and pomegranate seeds, onions, green chillies, chopped coriander, salt, flour and gram flour well. Add sufficient water and knead into a medium stiff dough. Cover with a damp cloth and set the dough aside for ten minutes.
3. Divide the dough into eight equal portions and shape into balls. Dust each ball lightly with flour and roll out into slightly thick *roti*.
4. Heat a non-stick *tawa*; place each *roti* on it and cook on medium heat. Turn the *roti* over after one minute and drizzle a little oil on it. Turn the *roti* over again and drizzle a little oil and cook till both sides are lightly golden.
5. Serve hot.

• **Preparation time:** 10-15 minutes • **Cooking time:** 20-25 minutes • **Serves:** 4

Bhature

Ingredients

3 cups refined flour (*maida*)
½ teaspoon baking powder
A pinch of soda bicarbonate
Salt to taste
½ cup yogurt
2 teaspoons sugar
2 teaspoons oil +
for deep-frying

Method

1. Sift together the flour, baking powder, soda bicarbonate and salt into a bowl.
2. Add the yogurt, sugar and one cup of water and knead into a soft dough. Add two teaspoons of oil and work it into the dough. Cover the dough with a damp cloth and set aside for thirty minutes.
3. Divide the dough into twenty portions and roll them into balls. Cover and set aside for fifteen minutes.
4. Grease your palms with oil and flatten each ball. Roll out each ball into a six-inch round *bhatura*.
5. Heat sufficient oil in a *kadai* and deep-fry each *bhatura*, turning sides till it puffs up and turns light brown in colour.
6. Drain on absorbent paper. Serve hot with Chhole (refer page 44).

• **Preparation time:** 1 hour • **Cooking time:** 40-45 minutes • **Serves:** 4

Accompaniments

Palm Court

होटल कनिष्क
Hotel Kanishka

Sookhi Dal

Ingredients

1 cup skinless split black gram (*dhuli urad dal*), soaked

1 teaspoon turmeric powder

Salt to taste

3 teaspoons ghee

1 teaspoon cumin seeds

1 medium onion, sliced

2 one-inch sticks cinnamon

3 green cardamoms

7-8 cloves

1 bay leaf

½ teaspoon black pepper powder

½ teaspoon sugar

For garnishing

2 teaspoons chopped fresh coriander

1 teaspoon lemon juice

Method

1. Drain and boil the *dal* in five cups of water, turmeric powder and salt till soft. Drain excess water and mash the *dal* lightly.
2. Heat the ghee in a non-stick pan; add the cumin seeds and when they change colour, add the onion and sauté till golden.
3. Add the cinnamon, cardamoms, cloves, bay leaf, pepper powder and sugar and sauté for a minute. Add the mashed *dal* and let it cook for five minutes on low heat.
4. Garnish with the chopped coriander and a sprinkling of lemon juice.
5. Serve hot with rice.

• **Preparation time:** 20-25 minutes • **Cooking time:** 20-25 minutes • **Serves:** 4

Dahi Kadhi

Ingredients

1 cup yogurt, whisked
¼ cup gram flour (*besan*)
½ teaspoon turmeric powder
1 teaspoon red chilli powder
Salt to taste
2 teaspoons oil
1 teaspoon cumin seeds
3 dried red chillies

For dumplings (*pakore*)
1 cup gram flour (*besan*)
1 medium onion, chopped
1 medium potato, chopped
1 teaspoon red chilli powder
1 teaspoon cumin powder
A pinch asafoetida
½ teaspoon baking powder
Salt to taste
Oil for deep-frying

Method

1. For the dumplings (*pakore*), combine the gram flour, onion, potato, chilli powder, cumin powder, asafoetida, baking powder, salt and sufficient water to form a thick batter of dropping consistency.
2. Heat sufficient oil in a *kadai*, drop spoonfuls of the batter into hot oil to make even-sized *pakore*. Deep-fry till golden brown and drain on absorbent paper. Set aside.
3. Whisk together the yogurt, gram flour, turmeric powder, chilli powder, salt and one cup of water to a smooth mixture.
4. Heat the oil in a non-stick pan and add the cumin seeds. When they change colour; add the red chillies and reduce heat. Add the yogurt mixture and stir briskly to prevent lumps from forming.
5. Increase the heat to medium and cook, stirring continuously, for five minutes.
6. Add the dumplings to the *kadhi* just before serving.
7. Serve hot with steamed rice.

• **Preparation time:** 20-25 minutes • **Cooking time:** 30-35 minutes • **Serves:** 4

Dal Makhni

Ingredients

½ cup whole black gram (*sabut urad*), soaked overnight

¼ cup red kidney beans (*rajma*), soaked overnight

2 teaspoons oil

2 teaspoons cumin seeds

1 teaspoon *garam masala* powder

2 tablespoons onion paste

2 teaspoons ginger-garlic paste

1 teaspoon turmeric powder

¼ cup tomato purée

1 teaspoon red chilli powder

Salt to taste

¼ cup butter

For garnishing

2 teaspoons fresh cream

2 teaspoons chopped fresh coriander

Method

1. Drain the black gram and kidney beans and put into a pressure cooker, Add four cups of water and cook under pressure till the pressure is released three to four times (three to four whistles). Open the lid when pressure is completely reduced. Drain, reserve the cooking liquid and set aside.
2. Heat the oil in a non-stick pan; add the cumin seeds and *garam masala* powder and sauté for a minute.
3. Add the onion paste, ginger-garlic paste and turmeric powder and sauté for half a minute. Add the tomato purée; mix and sauté for five minutes on medium heat.
4. Add the chilli powder and salt and sauté until mixture thickens. Add the black gram and kidney beans and mix well. Add the cooking liquid if the mixture is too thick.
5. Add the butter, stir and let the *dal* simmer on low heat for five minutes.
6. Remove from the heat, transfer into a serving bowl and garnish with the cream and chopped coriander. Serve hot.

• **Preparation time:** 20-25 minutes • **Cooking time:** 40-45 minutes • **Serves:** 4

Coriander Chutney

Coriander Chutney

Ingredients

1 cup roughly chopped fresh coriander

¾ cup roughly chopped fresh mint leaves

2 inches ginger, chopped

3 green chillies, chopped

1 lemon

½ teaspoon cumin seeds

Salt to taste

Method

1. Place chopped coriander, mint leaves, ginger, green chillies, freshly squeezed juice of lemon, cumin seeds and salt in a blender jar with two to three tablespoons of water and grind to a smooth paste. Transfer the chutney into a serving bowl.
2. Serve as an accompaniment to kababs or *samose*.

• **Preparation time:** 10-15 minutes

Mint Chutney

Ingredients

5 cups fresh mint, roughly chopped

3 cups fresh coriander, roughly chopped

10 green chillies, chopped

3 medium onions, peeled and roughly chopped

3 inches fresh ginger, peeled and roughly chopped

1 tablespoon lemon juice

Salt to taste

2 tablespoons pomegranate seed powder

Method

1. Grind the mint, coriander, green chillies, onions, and ginger to a fine paste, adding a little water if required. Add the lemon juice, salt and pomegranate seed powder. Mix well and serve.

• **Preparation time:** 10-15 minutes

Saunth

Ingredients

1 teaspoon dried ginger (*saunth*) powder

1 cup sugar

½ cup dried mango powder (*amchur*)

1 teaspoon white pepper powder

2 teaspoons red chilli powder

1 teaspoon black salt

⅓ teaspoon *garam masala* powder

⅓ teaspoon roasted cumin powder

⅓ teaspoon fennel (*saunf*) powder

Method

1. Mix the dried ginger powder, sugar, dried mango powder, white pepper powder, chilli powder, black salt, *garam masala* powder, cumin powder, fennel powder and three-fourth cup water to a smooth paste.
2. Pour into a non-stick pan and cook till the sugar dissolves completely. Stir and cook till the chutney thickens. Ensure that there are no lumps. Pass through a strainer and transfer into a serving dish. Chill and serve as an accompaniment.

• **Preparation time:** 15-20 minutes

Pineapple Raita

Ingredients

4 slices of canned pineapple

2 cups yogurt

Salt to taste

A pinch of roasted cumin powder

Method

1. Whisk the yogurt and salt together in a bowl. Chop the pineapple slices and add to the yogurt. Serve chilled, garnished with cumin powder.

• **Preparation time:** 15-20 minutes • **Serves:** 4

Irani Raita

Ingredients

3 medium cucumbers
2 cups yogurt, whisked
2 tablespoons honey
4 teaspoons raisins (*kishmish*), chopped
½ teaspoon white pepper powder
Salt to taste
1 teaspoon roasted cumin powder
2 tablespoons chopped fresh coriander

Method

1. Peel and finely chop the cucumbers. Place the yogurt in a deep bowl.
2. Add the cucumber, honey, raisins, white pepper powder and salt and mix well.
3. Sprinkle the cumin powder, garnish with the chopped coriander and serve chilled.

• **Preparation time:** 15-20 minutes • **Serves:** 4

Kashmiri Mooli Ka Raita

Ingredients

1 medium white radish (*mooli*), grated
2 cups yogurt
Salt to taste
2 green chillies, chopped
10 teaspoons chopped walnuts

Method

1. Place the grated radish in a piece of muslin, tie it up in a bundle and squeeze out the juice. Transfer the radish into a bowl.
2. Whisk the yogurt and salt in another bowl. Add the radish, green chillies and walnuts and mix well. Serve chilled, as an accompaniment to a meal.

• **Preparation time:** 20-25 minutes • **Serves:** 4

Sweet Mango Pickle

Ingredients

2 kg unripe green mangoes
1¼ kg grated jaggery
60 grams fenugreek (*methi dana*) powder
60 grams fennel (*saunf*) powder
25 grams onion seeds (*kalonji*)
25 grams caraway seeds (*shahi jeera*)
25 grams white pepper powder
25 grams black pepper powder
25 grams green cardamom powder
20 grams cinnamon powder
25 grams carom seed (*ajwain*) powder
25 grams dried ginger powder (*saunth*)
20 grams clove powder
20 grams asafoetida (hing)
250 ml vinegar
125 seedless dates, chopped
125 grams chopped onions
125 grams chopped garlic
200 grams sugar
60 grams red chilli powder
60 grams turmeric powder
60 grams salt
125 grams almonds, chopped
750 ml mustard oil

Method

1. Wash and wipe the mangoes completely dry before cutting each mango into four to six pieces.
2. Put the remaining ingredients with the mustard oil into a large sterilised jar. Put the mango pieces in the jar and shake it well. Cover the jar tightly and keep it in the sun for fifteen to twenty days or till the pickle matures.
3. Shake the contents of the container thoroughly once a day for even pickling of mango pieces. Serve as and when required.

Cauliflower, Turnip And Carrot Pickle

Ingredients

3 kg cauliflower, separated into florets
2 kg turnips, chopped
2 kg carrots, chopped
1 kg grated jaggery
1 litre vinegar
½ litre mustard oil
4 teaspoons Kashmiri red chilli powder
250 grams mustard powder
2 teaspoons red chilli powder
125 grams *garam masala* powder
250 grams onions, chopped
250 grams ginger, chopped
250 grams garlic, chopped
250 grams salt

Method

1. Place the cauliflower, turnips and carrots in sufficient boiling water for ten minutes. Drain well and spread them on a towel and keep in the sunlight till dry.
2. Soak the jaggery in vinegar overnight. Strain through a metal strainer.
3. Heat the oil in large non-stick pan. Add the Kashmiri chilli powder for colour.
4. Add the jaggery-vinegar mixture, mustard powder, chilli powder, *garam masala* powder, onions, ginger, garlic, salt and vegetables and cook for five minutes. Remove the pan from heat and let the pickle cool.
5. Transfer the pickle into sterilised earthenware or glass containers and cover tightly. Keep them in the sun for a week to mature. Shake the containers well at least twice a day to let the spices mix well.
6. Serve as and when required.

Garlic Pickle

Ingredients

1 kg garlic cloves, peeled
375 ml mustard oil
1 teaspoon cumin powder
1 teaspoon carom seed (*ajwain*) powder
125 ml vinegar
Salt to taste
1 teaspoon turmeric powder
1 teaspoon mustard powder

Method

1. Heat the mustard oil in a large non-stick pan.
2. When the oil starts smoking take the pan off the heat.
3. Once the oil cools slightly, add the cumin powder and carom seed powder and sauté till lightly browned.
4. Add the garlic cloves, vinegar, salt, turmeric powder, mustard powder and return the pan to heat.
5. Cook on medium heat for five minutes, stirring occasionally, till the garlic softens slightly. Remove the pan from the heat.
6. Allow the mixture to cool completely before storing in a sterilised container.

Sweets & Desserts

Palm Court

होटल कनिष्क
Hotel Kanishka

Besan Ke Laddoo

Ingredients

4 cups gram flour (*besan*)
2 cups ghee
2 teaspoons green cardamom powder
10-12 almonds, chopped
2 cups powdered sugar

Method

1. Heat the ghee in a non-stick *kadai* on low heat. Add the gram flour and sauté, stirring continuously, till the flour turns golden brown and fragrant. This could take about twenty minutes.
2. Add the cardamom powder, almonds and mix well. Remove the pan from heat and let the mixture cool. Add the powdered sugar and mix well.
3. Grease your palms, take small portions of mixture and shape into small round *laddoo*. Serve or store in an airtight container in a cool place.

• **Preparation time:** 10-15 minutes • **Cooking time:** 45-50 minutes • **Serves:** 4

Nutty Laddoo

Ingredients

2 cups shelled peanuts
2 cups cashew nuts
2 cups grated jaggery
1 teaspoon green cardamom powder
1 teaspoon freshly grated coconut
2 teaspoons ghee + for greasing

Method

1. Roast the peanuts, cool and remove the skins. Coarsely grind the peanuts and cashew nuts. Heat two teaspoons of water and the jaggery in a non-stick pan. Cook, stirring continuously, till the jaggery melts and turns into a syrup.
2. Add the ground peanut-cashew nut mixture, cardamom powder, coconut and ghee to the jaggery syrup and mix well.
3. Grease your palms with the ghee and shape the mixture, while still warm, into round *laddoo*. Cool and serve or store in an airtight container.

• **Serves:** 4 • **Preparation time:** 15-20 minutes • **Cooking time:** 1 hour

Besan ke Laddoo

Imarti

Ingredients

⅓ cup skinless split black gram (*dhuli urad dal*)

1 tablespoon cornflour

A few drops of edible orange food colour

1 cup sugar

2 teaspoons milk

A few saffron threads (*kesar*)

A few drops of screw pine essence (*kewda jal*)

Ghee for deep-frying

Method

1. Soak the *dal* for about two to three hours in two cups of water.
2. Drain and grind with the cornflour, orange food colour and one-fourth cup plus one tablespoon water to a fine batter, with consistency like that of cake batter. Set aside for one hour.
3. Cook the sugar with one cup of water, stirring, till the sugar dissolves. Add the milk and when the scum rises to the top, collect it with a ladle and discard. Cook till a syrup of one-string consistency is formed. Remove from heat; add the saffron and *kewda jal* and keep the syrup warm.
4. Heat sufficient ghee in a flat-bottomed pan meant specially for frying *imarti*.
5. Pour the *dal* paste into a cloth piping bag and pipe out the paste directly into the hot ghee in a circle and then overlapping with smaller circles on the border.
6. Deep-fry the *imarti* for three to four minutes on each side until they are golden.
7. Drain and immerse them in the warm syrup and let them soak for four to five minutes.
8. Remove the *imarti* from the syrup and drain excess syrup and arrange them in a serving plate. Serve the *imarti* hot.

• **Preparation time:** 1 hour plus • **Cooking time:** 30-35 minutes • **Serves:** 4

Moong Dal Ka Halwa

Ingredients

1 cup skinless split green gram (*dhuli moong dal*), soaked
1 cup sugar
1 cup ghee
¾ cup grated *khoya/mawa*
½ teaspoon green cardamom powder
4-5 almonds, slivered
6-7 cashew nuts, chopped

Method

1. Drain the *dal* and grind with very little water to a smooth paste.
2. Boil the sugar with two cups of water in a deep non-stick pan, till a syrup of one-thread consistency is formed.
3. Heat the ghee in a non-stick *kadai* on medium heat. Add the *dal* paste and sauté, stirring continuously, till the paste begins to turn golden brown in colour and the ghee starts to separate.
4. Add the sugar syrup and mix well. Cook on medium heat for five to seven minutes, stirring continuously. Add the *khoya* and keep stirring till the *khoya* blends well.
5. Add the cardamom powder, almonds and cashew nuts and continue cooking for another two minutes. Transfer the *halwa* into a serving bowl and serve hot.

• **Preparation time:** 1 hour • **Cooking time:** 40-45 minutes • **Serves:** 4

Badam Ka Halwa

Ingredients

3 cups almonds (*badam*)
1¼ cups ghee
¾ cup milk
¾ cup powdered sugar
A few saffron threads (*kesar*)
8-10 pistachios, chopped

Method

1. Soak the almonds in two cups of water overnight. Drain, peel and blend the almonds coarsely without adding water in a blender.
2. Heat the ghee in a non-stick *kadai*; add the almonds and sauté on low heat, stirring continuously, till the paste turns golden.
3. Stir in the milk and sugar and mix well. When the milk comes to a boil, reduce heat and cook, stirring continuously, till the milk is reduced to half its original volume.
4. Remove from heat and cover with a lid and let it rest for five minutes. Serve hot decorated with saffron and pistachios.

• **Preparation time:** 10-15 minutes • **Cooking time:** 40-45 minutes • **Serves:** 4

Gajar Ka Halwa

Ingredients

750 grams carrots, grated
¼ cup ghee
1 litre (5 cups) milk
2 cups sugar
1 cup grated *khoya/mawa*
½ teaspoon green cardamom powder
6-7 almonds, slivered
6-7 cashew nuts, chopped

Method

1. Heat half the ghee in a deep non-stick *kadai*; add the carrots and sauté for two to three minutes.
2. Add the milk, mix well and cook till all the milk is absorbed. Add the sugar and stir till it dissolves.
3. Add the *khoya* and keep stirring till the *khoya* blends well with the *halwa*. Add the cardamom powder, almonds, cashew nuts and the remaining ghee. Mix and cook for three to four minutes.
4. Transfer the *gajar ka halwa* into a serving bowl and serve hot.

• **Preparation time:** 25-30 minutes • **Cooking time:** 40-45 minutes • **Serves:** 4

Lavang Latika

Ingredients

Pastry

1 cup refined flour (*maida*)

3 tablespoons ghee + for deep-frying

Syrup

1 cup sugar

2 teaspoons milk

12 cloves

Stuffing

½ cup cottage cheese (*paneer*)

½ cup *khoya/mawa*, crumbled

6-8 almonds, slivered

8-10 pistachios, slivered

½ teaspoon clove powder

6 teaspoons powdered sugar

Method

1. For the pastry, place the flour in a bowl and rub in three tablespoons ghee. Add sufficient water and knead into a stiff dough. Cover with a damp cloth and let it rest for twenty to twenty-five minutes.
2. For the syrup, cook the sugar with half a cup of water, stirring till the sugar dissolves. Add the milk and when the scum rises to the top, collect it with a ladle and discard. Further cook the syrup till it reaches one-string consistency. Remove from heat and keep warm.
3. For the stuffing, mix together the cottage cheese, *khoya*, almonds, pistachios, clove powder and powdered sugar. Divide into twelve equal portions.
4. Divide the dough into twelve equal portions. Roll out each portion into a five-inch diameter *puri*.
5. Place one portion of the stuffing in the centre of each *puri*, fold in the sides to overlap each other and seal the ends with a little water. Secure with a clove.
6. Heat sufficient ghee in a *kadai* and deep-fry the *lavang latika* till golden brown. Drain on absorbent paper.
7. Soak the *lavang latika* in the warm sugar syrup for three to four minutes.
8. Drain and serve warm.

• **Preparation time:** 1 hour • **Cooking time:** 30-35 minutes • **Serves:** 4

Kulfi

Ingredients

7 cups milk
A few saffron threads (*kesar*)
½ cup sugar
A pinch of green cardamom powder
8-10 pistachios, chopped
8-10 cashew nuts, chopped

Method

1. Soak the saffron in one tablespoon of water. Heat the milk in a deep non-stick pan on medium heat, stirring continuously, till it is reduced to one-fourth of its original volume. Remove the milk from heat and add sugar and stir till the sugar is dissolved.
2. Add the cardamom powder, soaked saffron, pistachios and cashew nuts and mix well. Pour the mixture into the *kulfi* moulds and screw on the lids. Use a little dough to seal the sides of the mould lids. Keep the moulds in the freezer for two to three hours or till well set.
3. Before serving, dip bottom of the moulds in hot water for a few seconds. This will make it easier to remove the *kulfi* from the moulds. Invert *kulfi* onto a serving plate and serve immediately with Falooda (see below).

• **Preparation time:** 2 hours • **Cooking time:** 30-35 minutes • **Serves:** 4

Falooda

Mix ½ cup cornflour with two cups of water till smooth. Cook on low heat, stirring continuously, till the mixture thickens and become gelatinous.

Remove from heat and pour the mixture into a *falooda* press. Place the press over a container filled with cold water and press the mixture out in a continuous stream. Keep removing the *falooda* from the water and replenish the cold water if required.

Store *falooda* in a refrigerator. The *falooda* can be flavoured with screw pine essence or rose water. Serve the *falooda* chilled, as an accompaniment to Kulfi (see above).

• **Preparation time:** 10-15 minutes • **Cooking time:** 15-20 minutes • **Serves:** 4

Aval Payasam

Ingredients

¼ cup beaten rice (*poha*)
5 cups whole milk
1 cup sugar
½ teaspoon green cardamom powder
10 raisins (*kishmish*), chopped
4 teaspoons chopped cashew nuts
5 almonds, slivered
5 pistachios, slivered

Method

1. Wash and drain the *poha* and set aside to dry for ten minutes. Separate the grains with a fork.
2. Heat the milk in a deep non-stick pan. When the milk starts boiling, add the *poha* and mix well. Reduce the heat and cook, stirring continuously, till it is reduced to half its original volume.
3. Add the sugar, cardamom powder, raisins and cashew nuts and mix. Simmer for five to ten minutes before removing from heat. Transfer the *payasam* into a serving dish and decorate with the almonds and pistachios. Serve hot or warm.

• **Preparation time:** 15-20 minutes • **Cooking time:** 20-25 minutes • **Serves:** 4

Gulab Jamun

Ingredients

1½ cups *khoya/mawa*
¼ cup cottage cheese (*chhena/paneer*)
7 teaspoons refined flour (*maida*)
¼ teaspoon green cardamom powder
2 cups sugar
A few saffron threads (*kesar*)
Ghee for deep-frying

Method

1. Heat the sugar in a non-stick pan with two cups of water and bring to a boil. Keep removing the scum, if any and cook till it turns a light golden. Add the saffron and keep the sugar syrup warm.

2. Grate the *khoya* and mash the *chenna*. Mix both with the flour, cardamom powder and a little water to make a soft dough.
3. Divide the dough into sixteen equal portions and shape into balls.
4. Heat sufficient ghee in a *kadai*. Slide in the balls gently and deep-fry on low heat till they turn golden. Drain and soak them in the warm sugar syrup for at least twenty minutes before serving.

Note: *Khoya/mawa* used for gulab jamun is of a special kind known as chikna khoya. Loose and sticky in consistency and yellowish in colour, it is made by reducing low-fat milk.

• **Preparation time:** 30-35 minutes • **Cooking time:** 30-35 minutes • **Serves:** 4

Phirni

Ingredients

1 litre (5 cups) milk
¼ cup Basmati rice, soaked
1 cup sugar
A few saffron threads (*kesar*)
1 teaspoon green cardamom powder
A few drops of rose water
4-5 pistachios, blanched and chopped
4-5 almonds, blanched and slivered

Method

1. Drain the water and grind the rice with a little water to a fine paste.
2. Bring the milk to a boil in a deep non-stick pan; add the rice paste and cook on low heat, stirring continuously for ten to fifteen minutes.
3. Add the sugar and continue to cook, stirring continuously, until the mixture thickens to a custard-like consistency. Add the saffron, cardamom powder and rose water and mix. Remove from heat.
4. Pour into individual bowls, decorate with the pistachios and almonds. Allow to cool and then place in the refrigerator to chill. Serve chilled.

• **Preparation time:** 25-30 minutes • **Cooking time:** 20-25 minutes • **Serves:** 4

Malpua

Ingredients

1 litre (5 cups) milk

300 grams sugar

1 gram saffron threads (*kesar*)

1 teaspoon screw pine essence (*kewda jal*)

2 tablespoons grated cottage cheese (*paneer*)

30 grams refined flour (*maida*)

1 teaspoon green cardamom powder

Ghee for deep-frying

4 teaspoons chopped pistachios

Rabdi (see below), as required

Method

1. Boil the milk in a heavy-bottomed non-stick pan till it is reduced and reaches a coating consistency. Cool and set aside.
2. Reserve thirty grams of sugar and cook the rest with half cup of water to make a sugar syrup of one-string consistency. Soak the saffron in a teaspoon of hot milk and add it to the sugar syrup. Add the *kewda jal* and mix.
3. Add the cottage cheese, refined flour, reserved sugar and cardamom powder to the cooled milk. Mix well and make a batter of pouring consistency, adding a little milk if required. Set aside for three hours.
4. Heat the ghee in a wide-mouthed flat-bottomed *kadai*. Pour a little batter to form a pancake. Pour hot ghee over it and turn over. When both sides are properly done, drain and immerse in the sugar syrup. Soak the *malpua* in the syrup for five to ten minutes. Remove the *malpua* from the syrup and fold into half or in triangular shape. Arrange them on a serving plate and serve hot, decorated with the pistachios and *rabdi*.

• **Preparation time:** 3 hours plus • **Cooking time:** 30-35 minutes • **Serves:** 4

Rabdi

Heat 1½ litres (7½ cups) milk in a deep non-stick pan on medium heat, stirring continuously till the milk is reduced to one-fifth its original volume. Add ½ cup sugar and a pinch of green cardamom powder and stir till the sugar is dissolved.

Allow to cool a little and add ½ cup grated cottage cheese and continue to stir till the cottage cheese blends well with the milk. Keep in the refrigerator to chill. Serve, decorated with a few threads of saffron, 4-5 chopped pistachios and 3-4 drops of screw pine essence (*kewda jal*).

• **Preparation time:** 8-10 minutes • **Cooking time:** 35-40 minutes • **Serves:** 4

Shahi Tukre

Ingredients

8 slices white bread
1 cup ghee
2 litres (10 cups) milk
½ cup sugar
1 teaspoon green cardamom powder
A few saffron threads (*kesar*)
6-8 almonds, slivered
6-8 pistachios, chopped

Method

1. Heat the ghee in a deep *kadai* and deep-fry the bread slices. Drain on absorbent paper.
2. To make the condensed milk, heat the milk in a deep non-stick pan and when it comes to a boil, reduce heat and simmer till it is reduced to one-third its original volume.
3. Stir in the sugar, cardamom powder and half the saffron. Remove from heat and set aside to cool.
4. Add the fried bread slices to the condensed milk and let them soak for ten to fifteen minutes. Carefully lift the slices from the milk so that they do not break and place them on a serving platter.
5. Pour the remaining condensed milk on the slices, decorate with the almonds, pistachios and the remaining saffron. Place in the refrigerator to chill and serve. Alternatively, serve at room temperature.

• **Preparation time:** 15-20 minutes • **Cooking time:** 1 hour • **Serves:** 4

Table Service

Basics of table service

Grace, style and observance of custom can enhance the quality of a meal. A dish may be superbly cooked with the flavours enhanced by giving the guests personal attention, attending to their needs promptly and ensuring that the service is correct.

There are some basic rules to be followed for the service at the table, depending on the comfort of the guest. All food is served from the left of the guest. All beverages are served from the right. The elderly, women and children are to be served first. Dishes are cleared from the right and dishes are not stacked in the presence of the guest.

Table settings

A well-made dish deserves to be served in an appealing manner, with a grace and style that enhances the occasion. The table settings should be done in a manner that is appealing to the guests' eye. Table settings include the basics such as tablecloths, napkins, crockery, cutlery and other necessities.

The following table setting is recommended for a lunch or dinner service. A clean tablecloth should cover the table, extending a minimum of 12 inches over the table's edge, yet not hindering the guests' level of comfort.

A "cover" - a guest's plate, silverware, glass and napkin - should be set on the table. This includes a folded napkin in the centre of the cover (and ¼ inch from the table's edge), two dinner forks to the left of the napkin, a dinner knife, a bread-and-butter knife (the cutting edge facing the plate) and two teaspoons to the right of the napkin in 1, 2, 3, 4 order. All silverware to be placed ¼ inch from the table edge.

The bread-and-butter plate should be at least 1 inch above the fork tines. The water glass, bottom up, is to be placed slightly to the right of the tip of the dinner knife.

This setting places all the silverware needed by the guest except for the soup (with which the essential silver is served) on the table ahead of the guests' arrival.

The silverware, whether used or not used, is removed with the plates after the course is completed.

The water glass is turned over and filled with water as soon as the guest is seated.

Types of glasses

Some of the commonly used glasses are as follows:

Champagne: The most common type is the saucer that holds about 12 oz. The tulip-shaped glass is popular as it shows off the bubbles better and holds the sparkle longer.

Wine: In sizes ranging from 5 to 10 oz. The top and bowl are medium size and the glass is slightly deeper than wide.

Cocktail: Cocktail glasses come in many sizes and shapes. The standard glass has a wide top, shallow bowl, and holds 3 to 4 oz. However, for cocktails "on the rocks" the 5 to 6 oz. goblet is popular.

Large Brandy Snifter: Resembles an over-sized electric light bulb on a stem and holds 6 to 8 oz. but is never filled.

Tom Collins: This large cylindrical glass resembles an ordinary water glass and usually holds 12 oz.

Liqueur Glass: A short-stemmed, tulip-shaped glass holding 3 oz. with or without a line at the 1 oz. level.

Wine service

White wines are served chilled while red wines are generally served at room temperature. Traditionally, white wines are served with white meats and red wines with red meat.

Presentation of the bottle to a guest is an important part of the culture of serving wines. Opening of the wine bottle begins with the removal of the foil around the cork and neck of the bottle. The foil should be removed with a knife. Set the corkscrew into the cork and turn it carefully all the way down the cork. Pour a few drops of the wine into a glass for the guest's approval.

White wine glasses should not be filled more than three-fourth full. Red wine glasses are generally larger than white wine glasses and should be filled only one-half to two-third full. Red wine should be handled carefully and be served without shaking or turning the bottle. This is because red wine often produces sediment with age and maturity.

Measurements

Ingredients	Quantity/No	Weight
Almonds	10	15 grams
Apple	1 medium	120 grams
Asafoetida (*hing*)	1 teaspoon	4 grams
Asafoetida (*hing*)	1 pinch	0.25 gram
Baking powder	1 teaspoon	3 grams
Basmati rice	1 cup	200 grams
Bay leaf	1	0.4 gram
Bengal gram split (*chana dal*)	1 cup	200 grams
Black cardamom powder	1 teaspoon	2 grams
Black cardamoms	11	10 grams
Black pepper powder	1 teaspoon	3 grams
Black peppercorns	5	1 gram
Black peppercorns	1 cup	100 grams
Black salt	1 teaspoon	5 grams
Boneless skinless chicken breast	1	65 grams
Bottle gourd	1 medium	500 grams
Bottle gourd	1 small	250 grams
Breadcrumbs	1 cup	110 grams
Breadcrumbs	2 tablespoons	12 grams
Brinjal (round), large	1	460 grams
Brinjal (round), medium	1	275 grams
Brinjal, big	1	630 grams
Brinjal, medium	1	30 grams
Brinjal, small	9	240 grams
Broccoli, small florets	5	15 grams
Butter	1 tablespoon	15 grams
Cabbage, small	1	150 grams
Caraway seeds (*shahi jeera*)	1 teaspoon	3 grams
Carom seeds (*ajwain*)	1 teaspoon	2 grams

Ingredients	Quantity/No	Weight
Carrot, grated	1 cup	150 grams
Carrot, medium	1	90 grams
Carrot, small	1	48 grams
Cashew nut paste	1 cup	225 grams
Cashew nut paste	1 tablespoon	15 grams
Cashew nuts	10	20 grams
Cashew nuts, coarsely powdered	1 cup	125 grams
Caster sugar	1 cup	125 grams
Cauliflower, medium	1	500 grams
Chaat masala	1 teaspoon	1 gram
Cheese	1 cup, grated	80 grams
Chicken drumstick	1	125 grams
Chicken drum-sticks (with bone)	8	500 grams
Chicken mince	1 cup	250 grams
Chickpeas	2 tablespoons	30 grams
Chickpeas	½ cup	100 grams
Cinnamon	1 inch	0.5 gram
Cinnamon powder	1 teaspoon	2 grams
Cloves	10	1 gram
Coconut milk	1 cup	200 ml
Cooked rice (plain)	1 cup	150 grams
Coriander powder	1 teaspoon	2 grams
Coriander seeds (*sabut dhania*)	1 tablespoon	6 grams
Cornflour	1 tablespoon	5 grams
Cornmeal (*makai atta*)	1 tablespoon	10 grams
Cottage cheese (*paneer*), grated	½ cup	70 grams
Crab	1	300 grams
Cucumber, medium	1	125 grams
Cucumber, small	1	75 grams
Cumin powder	1 teaspoon	3 grams
Cumin seeds	1 teaspoon	3 grams

Ingredients	Quantity/No	Weight
Curry leaves	10	1 gram
Dates	1 cup	200 grams
Dried fenugreek leaves (*kasoori methi*)	1 tablespoon	1 gram
Dried mango powder (*amchur*)	1 teaspoon	1 gram
Dried pomegranate seeds	1 teaspoon	3 grams
Dried red chillies	10	20 grams
Egg	1 (small)	50 grams
Egg	1 (big)	75 grams
Fennel seeds (*saunf*)	1 teaspoon	3 grams
Fennel seeds (*saunf*) powder	1 teaspoon	3 grams
Fenugreek leaves	1 small bunch	175 grams
Fenugreek leaves	1 medium bunch	250 grams
Fenugreek leaves	1 large bunch	580 grams
Fenugreek seeds	1 teaspoon	5 grams
Fenugreek seeds	1 tablespoon	12 grams
Fenugreek seeds powder	1 teaspoon	5 grams
French beans	10	75 grams
Fresh button mushrooms	10 medium	125 grams
Fresh coriander leaves	1 cup	25 grams
Fresh coriander leaves	1 small bunch	100 grams
Fresh coriander leaves	1 medium bunch	200 grams
Fresh coriander leaves	1 large bunch	550 grams
Fresh coriander leaves, chopped	1 tablespoon	5 grams
Fresh cream	1 cup	200 ml
Fresh cream	4 tablespoons	60 ml
Fresh green peas, shelled	1 cup	150 grams
Fresh green peas, shelled	1 tablespoon	10 grams
Fresh mint leaves	1 cup	30 grams

Ingredients	Quantity/No	Weight
Fresh mint leaves	1 small bunch	70 grams
Fresh mint leaves	1 medium bunch	120 grams
Fresh mint leaves	1 large bunch	205 grams
Fresh mint leaves, chopped	1 tablespoon	4 grams
Fresh pomegranate kernels	1 cup	180 grams
Fresh pomegranate kernels	1 tablespoon	10 grams
Fresh grated coconut	1 cup	120 grams
Fresh grated coconut	1 tablespoon	5 grams
Fresh yeast	1 tablespoon	10 grams
Garam masala powder	1 teaspoon	2 grams
Garlic	10 cloves	15 grams
Garlic paste	1 tablespoon	15 grams
Ghee	1 tablespoon	15 grams
Ghee	1 cup	210 grams
Ginger	1 inch	10 grams
Ginger paste	1 tablespoon	15 grams
Gram flour (*besan*)	1 tablespoon	5 grams
Gram flour (*besan*)	1 cup	100 grams
Green capsicum, medium	1	125 grams
Green capsicum, small	1	98 grams
Green cardamom powder	1 teaspoon	2 grams
Green cardamoms	10	3 grams
Green chilli	1	2 grams
Green chilli paste	1 teaspoon	5 grams
Green chutney	2 tablespoons	27 grams
Green chutney	¼ cup	48 grams
Green mango	1 small	100 grams
Honey	1 tablespoon	15 ml
Hung yogurt	1 cup	275 grams
Jaggery, grated	1 cup	200 grams
Jaggery, grated	1 teaspoon	10 grams
Jaggery, grated	1 tablespoon	30 grams

Ingredients	Quantity/No	Weight
Ladies' fingers	40 medium	300 grams
Lemon juice	1 teaspoon	5 ml
Mace	2 blades	3 grams
Mace powder	a pinch	0.08 gram
Mawa/khoya, grated	1 cup	180 grams
Mawa/khoya, grated	1 tablespoon	20 grams
Melon seeds (*magaz*)	3 tablespoons	32 grams
Milk	1 cup	200 ml
Minced mutton	1 cup	250 grams
Mustard powder	1 teaspoon	3 grams
Mustard seeds	1 teaspoon	4 grams
Mustard seeds	1 tablespoon	10 grams
Nutmeg powder	1 teaspoon	2 grams
Onion seeds (*kalonji*)	1 teaspoon	3 grams
Onion, large	1	110 grams
Onion, medium	1	90 grams
Onion, small	1	60 grams
Orange	1 medium	150 grams
Papaya paste	3 tablespoons	25 grams
Peanuts	1 tablespoon	10 grams
Peanuts	1 cup	200 grams
Pineapple	1 slice	50 grams
Pistachios	20	10 grams
Pistachios	¼ cup	30 grams
Pomfret fillets, large	2	225 grams
Pomfret fillets, small	8	200 grams
Pomfret, medium	1	220 grams
Poppy seeds (*khus khus*)	1 teaspoon	4 grams
Potato, large	1	150 grams
Potato, medium	1	100 grams
Powdered sugar	1 cup	125 grams
Prawns, large	24	360 grams
Prawns, medium	32	300 grams
Prawns, small	30	250 grams

Ingredients	Quantity/No	Weight
Pure ghee/*desi* ghee	1 cup	225 grams
Radish	1 medium	80 grams
Raisins (white/ black)	10	5 grams
Raisins (white/ black)	½ cup	90 grams
	1 tablespoon	12 grams
Red chilli paste	1 teaspoon	7 grams
Red chilli powder	1 teaspoon	3 grams
Red chilli powder	1 cup	100 grams
Red kidney beans (*rajma*)	1½ cups	275 grams
Refined flour (*maida*)	1 cup	120 grams
Refined flour (*maida*)	2 tablespoons	15 grams
Rice	1 cup	200 grams
Roasted cumin powder	1 teaspoon	3 grams
Roasted peanuts	2 tablespoons	18 grams
Roasted peanuts	¼ cup	30 grams
Salt	1 teaspoon	5 grams
Sarson ka saag	1 bunch	500 grams
Semolina (*rawa/ suji*)	1 cup	200 grams
Semolina (*rawa/ suji*)	1 tablespoon	13 grams
Sesame seeds	1 cup	160 grams
Sesame seeds (*til*)	1 teaspoon	5 grams
Soda bicarbonate	1 teaspoon	4 grams
Spinach leaves	10	60 grams
Spinach leaves	1 small bunch	150 grams
Spinach leaves	1 medium bunch	250 grams
Spinach leaves	1 large bunch	450 grams
Split Bengal gram (*chana dal*)	1 teaspoon	5 grams
Split Bengal gram (*chana dal*)	1 cup	200 grams
Split pigeon pea (*toovar dal/ arhar dal*)	1 cup	200 grams

Ingredients	Quantity/No	Weight
Split pigeon pea (toovar dal/ arhar dal)	1 teaspoon	5 grams
Split red lentils (*masoor dal*)	1 cup	200 grams
Split skinless black gram (*dhuli urad dal*)	1 teaspoon	5 grams
Skinless split black gram (*dhuli urad dal*)	1 teaspoon	5 grams
Skinless split black gram (*dhuli urad dal*)	1 cup	200 grams
Skinless split green gram (*dhuli moong dal*)	1 cup	200 grams
Spring onions bulbs without greens	2	20 grams
Spring onions with greens	2	100 grams
Sprouted moong	½ cup	50 grams
Star anise	2	4 grams
Sugar	1 tablespoon	15 grams
Sugar	1 cup	250 grams
Sugar	1 teaspoon	5 grams
Sweet date and tamarind chutney	¼ cup	60 grams
Tamarind chutney	2 tablespoons	38 grams

Ingredients	Quantity/No	Weight
Tamarind pulp	1 teaspoon	5 grams
Tamarind pulp	1 tablespoon	20 grams
Tomato purée, fresh	1 tablespoon	15 grams
Tomato purée, fresh	1 cup	235 grams
Tomato purée, packaged	1 cup	280 grams
Tomato, large	1	110 grams
Tomato, medium	1	95 grams
Tomato, small	1	60 grams
Turmeric powder (*haldi*)	1 tablespoon	9 grams
Turmeric powder (*haldi*)	1 teaspoon	3 grams
Vinegar	1 tablespoon	15 ml
Walnuts	1 cup	120 grams
White bread	8 slices	210 grams
White pepper powder	1 teaspoon	3 grams
Whole black gram (*sabut urad dal*)	1 cup	250 grams
Whole chicken	1	800 grams
Whole-wheat flour (*atta*)	1 cup	150 grams
Yogurt	1 cup	250 grams
Yogurt, thick	4 tablespoons	75 grams

Glossary

English	Hindi
Almonds	Badam
Arrowroot	Paniphal, Tikora
Asafoetida	Hing
Bay leaf	Tej patta
Beaten rice	Poha/chewra
Bengal gram, split	Chana dal
Black cardamoms	Badi elaichi
Black gram, skinless split	Dhuli urad dal
Black gram, whole	Sabut urad
Black peppercorns	Kali mirch
Black salt	Kala namak
Bottle gourd	Lauki/ghia
Breadcrumbs	Bread ka choora
Button mushrooms	Kukurmutta/ Gucchi/Dhingri
Capsicum	Shimla mirch
Caraway seeds	Shahi jeera
Carom seeds	Ajwain
Cashew nuts	Kaju
Celery	Ajmud
Chicken, boneless	Murgh boti
Chicken, breasts	Murgh ka seena
Chicken, mince	Murgh ka keema
Chickpeas	Kabuli chana
Cinnamon	Dalchini
Clove	Laung
Coriander seeds	Sabut dhania
Cornmeal	Makai ka atta
Cottage cheese	Paneer
Crab	Kekda
Cucumber	Kakdi/Kheera
Cumin seeds	Jeera
Curry leaves	Kadhi patta/ meetha neem
Dates	Khajur
Dried fenugreek leaves	Kasoori methi
Dried ginger powder	Saunth
Dried mango powder	Amchur
Dried pomegranate seeds	Anardana
Dried red chillies	Sookhi lal mirch
Fennel seeds	Saunf
Fenugreek leaves	Methi
Fenugreek seeds	Methi dana
French beans	Farsi
Fresh coriander leaves	Hara dhania
Fresh cream	Malai
Fresh mint leaves	Pudina
Fresh mustard leaves	Sarson ka saag
Gram flour	Besan
Green cardamom	Chhoti elaichi

English	Hindi
Green gram, skinless split	Dhuli moong dal
Green peas	Hare matar
Honey	Shahad/madhu
Jaggery	Gur
Leek	Bilayti pyaaz
Lotus stem	Kamal kakdi/ Bhein/Nadru
Mace	Javitri
Mangoes, unripe green	Keri
Melon seeds	Magaz
Mustard seeds	Rai/sarson
Mutton/lamb, boneless	Gosht boti
Mutton/lamb, kidney	Gurda
Mutton/lamb, liver	Kaleji
Mutton/lamb, ribs	Pasliyan
Nutmeg	Jaiphal
Onion seeds	Kalonji
Orange	Narangi/santra
Papaya, unripe green	Kachcha papita
Peanuts/ground nuts	Moongphali
Pineapple	Annanas
Pistachio	Pista
Pomegranate kernels	Anar ke dane
Pomfret	Halva/saranga/ chandwa
Poppy seeds	Khus khus
Prawns	Jheenga
Radish	Mooli
Raisins	Kishmish
Red kidney beans	Rajma
Red lentils, split	Masoor dal
Refined flour	Maida
Rose water	Gulab jal
Saffron	Kesar
Screw pine water	Kewda jal
Semolina	Rawa/suji
Sesame, white	Safed til
Sole	Repti/morrul
Spinach	Palak
Star anise	Phool chakri/ badiyan
Tamarind	Imli
Turnip	Shalgam
Vetivier	Khus
Vinegar	Sirka
Walnut	Akhrot
Whole-wheat flour	Atta
Yeast	Khameer
Yogurt	Dahi
Yogurt, hung	Chakka